BEYOND HAPPINESS

BEYOND HAPPINESS

DEEPENING THE DIALOGUE BETWEEN BUDDHISM, PSYCHOTHERAPY AND THE MIND SCIENCES

Gay Watson

KARNAC

40.00

First published in 2008 by
Karnac Books Ltd
118 Finchley Road
London NW3 5HT

British Library Cataloguing in Publication Data

A.C.I.P. for this book is available from the British Library

ISBN-13: 978-1-85575-404-1

Edited, designed, and produced by Sheffield Typesetting
www.sheffieldtypesetting.com
e-mail: admin@ sheffieldtypesetting.com

www.karnacbooks.com

CONTENTS

ABOUT THE AUTHOR

Gay Watson, PhD, trained as a psychotherapist with the Karuna Institute of Core Process Psychotherapy, a Buddhist-inspired psychotherapy. Concurrently she attained a first class honours degree followed by a doctorate in the field of Buddhist Studies at the School of Oriental and African Studies of London University. She is the author of *Resonance of Emptiness: A Buddhist Inspiration for a Contemporary Psychotherapy* (Routledge Curzon, 1998. 2001 pb.) and co-editor of *The Psychology of Awakening* (UK: Rider, 1999; USA: Samuel Weiser, 2001). She is currently associated with the Karuna Institute and Sharpham College of Buddhism and Contemporary Inquiry, and a member of the editorial board of *Contemporary Buddhism*. She lives in Devon, UK, and is a Trustee of the Dartington Hall Trust.

PREFACE

May all beings have happiness and the causes of happiness.
May they all be free from suffering and the causes of suffering.
May they never be separate from the sacred happiness untainted by suffering.
May they abide in great impartiality, free from attachment to close ones and aversion to others.

* * *

In this book I will try to open out the discussion between Buddhist thought and psychotherapy and the new findings of neuroscience in the context of our search for wellbeing. Buddhist teachings are concerned with a way of living and engage most resonantly with practice rather than with theory, thus the conversation between Buddhism and psychotherapy has been a particularly fruitful one for as long as dialogue has existed between Buddhist and Western disciplines. In search of a way to happiness, Buddha set out to explore our experience and in so doing presented what may well be called the earliest "psychology", an experiential exploration of subjectivity. In the West, for much of the twentieth century, psychology (science) and psychotherapy (practice) had little to say to one another. Despite Sigmund Freud's early wish to consider psychoanalysis as a science, academic psychology had scant time for what it considered at best an "art" form, while psychotherapy found little of interest in psychology's lack of concern with subjective experience. All this has changed since the growth of the interdisciplinary fields of cognitive science, neuroscience and consciousness studies, and the development of new technology.

New technology and new scientific approaches have pushed forward the frontiers of knowledge about our own experience, and contemporary mind sciences are stumbling towards an ever-clearer picture of what it means to be human, revealing exciting facts about how our minds work as observed from an objective stance. These new discoveries about the brain and its development, damage and repair have much to teach us about health and happiness. The new knowledge challenges many of the common sense and folk psychology beliefs we have long held, as well as cherished philosophical and psychological views. Such knowledge calls for understanding and reflection, and then new action. It has important implications for education in the field of emotional intelligence, and illuminates how psychotherapy actually works. More surprisingly perhaps, its findings resonate with those of the "first" psychology. This is the moment to bring neuroscience into the long-established dialogue between psychotherapy and Buddhism, to explore a potential path informed by all three disciplines towards mental and physical health and happiness. Thus I am concerned with opening up a multi-faceted discussion between Buddhist thought and practice and the Western disciplines of mind sciences and psychotherapy. Above all, my attempt is to keep this discussion close to our experience.

I must first point out that while there are as many "Buddhisms" as Christian denominations, it is with the shared central core of teachings, and with a concern for these teachings (or Dharma) as a way of living rather than as any particular system, that I engage in this dialogue. For my own orientation, I own an adherence first to the Mahayana or later Buddhism, and a leaning towards Tibetan interpretations of this. From the Western perspective, I am a European woman who spends time in the United States, a wife, a mother, a scholar and a psychotherapist. I am not a scientist and freely admit that my understanding of these fields comes from secondary sources which report back to the interested layperson from the fields of research. My concern is with the implications of such research for psychotherapy and for everyday life. Thus inevitably I speak from these perspectives. Amid this, my aim—if it is not too paradoxical—is to find a ground *without* taking up a position.

At this time many of the presenting problems of those coming for therapy are concerned with issues of meaning and of self. While changes of view in science and philosophy might seem of little concern to ordinary lives, their effects filter down into the culture within which we live and by which we are constructed. Western thought has been undergoing a paradigm shift, which started in the last century with relativity, indeterminacy and quantum mechanics in the scientific field, with cubism and abstraction in art, stream of consciousness and fragmented narrative in writing, and deconstruction in theory. Both Western science and the humanities have encountered change, wherein their own discoveries have paradoxically proved hard to fit within earlier frameworks of understanding. From a negative perspective, this background of change has led to a loss of confidence in religion, society, even our selves. When the foundations of belief lose their validity, we need to look afresh at our experience and the ways in which, often unconsciously, we interpret it. On the positive front, it is these very changes in viewpoint, especially in science, which may lead to new possibilities. In particular, what has become known as complexity theory has had a powerful influence upon the very framework of science, giving sanction to exploration of conscious and non-conscious experience in a way unforeseen a generation earlier. It is this change in scientific outlook that brings it into more direct dialogue with Buddhist thought. This reframing of science rests broadly on a new vision of causality wherein consequences are seen as arising from networks of multiple and reciprocal causation rather than in linear fashion from a direct cause. This is an old idea for Buddhism, where the central theory is that of dependent co-arising. So today, ideas arising from Buddhism and from contemporary cognitive science may encourage us to engage anew with our experience, our embodiment and our relationships.

My discussion is loosely based on a traditional Tibetan Buddhist model. In the first section, *View*, I will begin by introducing the field of engagement: where we are now, and where we have come from in this conversation. Then I will present a chapter on contemporary explanations from neuroscience and consciousness studies, which will be followed by consideration of psychotherapy, psychology in action. This will lead into a brief outline of Buddhist thought.

In the middle or *Meditation* section I shall contemplate important aspects of our experience of embodiment, emotion, environment and our selves. Contemporary sciences of mind are exposing facts about these topics that challenge common sense views which have arisen from earlier beliefs, largely those of Cartesian and Newtonian frameworks. I will reflect on these topics, looking outwards from our subjective experience both to Buddhist ideas and to contemporary Western scientific findings. *Embodiment* will attempt to bring awareness to our moment-to-moment sensory experience, and will consider both our normal unawareness of this and the theoretical centrality of embodiment within the new findings of the mind sciences. *Emotion* will continue discussion of recent findings relating to emotion, particularly those concerning the healthy development of emotional self-regulation, and later-life repair for unhealthy development. It will also consider Buddhist views and practices as resources for psychotherapy and for emotional health. *Environment* will attempt to expand our personal awareness of embodiment and emotion into awareness of our interdependent participation with the natural world and the culture within which we are embedded. Neuroscience is increasingly concerned with the importance of situation, context and intersubjectivity, and this has important consequences in terms of our wellbeing. Since this is dependent upon others, it also depends on ethical conduct and recognition of the universal dimension of our actions. Thus throughout, the theme of ethics will recur, as grounded in our embodiment, as affected by our emotions, and perhaps most strongly, as ethics of human ecology. Finally in this section, *Self and non-self* will consider the implications of the preceding chapters for our views of our selves.

In the last section, *Action*, I will suggest new dispositions of action and communication that may help us to incorporate and instantiate these findings, enabling us to forge new relationships with our embodiment, emotion and environment, ourselves and others. I will consider both awareness and the feminine voice and imagination and creativity as inspiring different ways of being and understanding.

I would like to acknowledge profound gratitude to Stephen Batchelor for his continuing support and discussions over the years, and to Bridget McCrum and Fran Gyn for visual and coastal adventures and for liberating me, at least for a while, from the word. My thanks also go to Paul Broks for support and scientific reading, and to all of those authors whose works I have turned to in informing my own synthesis, any errors in which are, of course, mine alone. Above all, my thanks go to David, who read it, and to my friends and family. I also gratefully acknowledge the importance of place, the two spaces in Devon and Marin County, California which have nurtured thought and writing.

PART I
VIEW

CHAPTER ONE

View from within and without: first and third person perspectives

Happiness is the original true nature of all being. The word itself affords me some confidence in this theory. Happiness does not mean joy. The word is related to "happen", which comes from the Middle English "hap"—chance, fortune, that which occurs. Haps are what happen, and so happiness amounts to a shortened form of the very happeningness of the world. The nature of happiness, in other words, is the happiness of Nature.

(Daniel, 2005)

God, grant me the serenity to accept the things I cannot change, the courage to change the things I can, and the wisdom to know the difference.[1]

The secret of happiness (and therefore of success) is to be in harmony with existence, to be always calm, always lucid, always willing, "to be joined to the universe without being more conscious of it than an idiot", to let each wave of life wash us a little farther up the shore.

(Connolly, 1944, p. 15)

One day I was riding down the lane beyond my house. It was a cold winter's day with bright sun after a freezing night. Coming round a bend in the track, suddenly the winter sunlight was shining through the frosted hedgerow. Each frost crystal became a diamond, the track a jewelled tunnel shining in the sun. It was breathtaking. As my horse walked through this glory, I turned to try and catch a last glimpse, but then I was facing in the other direction, the sun was behind me and I was between the sun and the crystal. All that remained was a damp green brown hedgerow, winter bare, no sparkle, all glory gone. I have never forgotten that moment. It showed how dependent we are on where we are looking from. It was the same hedge in the same landscape, but it was also a different experience. Only much later did I realise that the wonder faded as I changed my position in such a way that I was in the way, between sun and object. That seems symbolic. It is so often that we get in the way, that the image gets in the way of the process.

As I touch my happiness, I see the world differently. Locked in sorrow, it's hard to enjoy the sunshine. As Wittgenstein wrote, "The world of the happy man is a different one from that of the unhappy man" (1961, p. 149). As we become aware of how the way we actually view the world day to day is dependent upon our feelings, we also see that those feelings themselves have been formed by earlier experience. How can we intervene in the cycle? Is there something we can do to foster wellbeing and happiness, see the diamonds rather than the mud?

All life is suffering or unsatisfactory. This fact should be thoroughly known. So says the first ennobling truth of Buddhism. This seems at first glance unduly dismal, and is probably responsible for the early reception of Buddhism as a pessimistic religion. However, let us look more closely.

Everyone desires wellbeing. This is also the unstated foundation of the Buddha's fundamental four truths. Life is unsatisfactory because our search for happiness is always thwarted—by sorrow, by illness, by the sheer impermanence and change of things, and most finally by death. The remaining three truths, which we will look at in more detail later, concern the cause of suffering, the possibility of the cessation of suffering, and the path to such cessation. All of these emphasise that anguish is neither what we want nor inevitable. The bottom line for Buddhism and for all of us, in the words of perhaps its most high-profile contemporary exponent, His Holiness the Dalai Lama (1998), is that we "desire happiness and wish to avoid suffering". This has been stated more dryly in neurological terms: "The attempt to regulate affect—to minimize unpleasant feelings and to maximize pleasant ones—is the driving force in human motivation" (Westen, 1997, quoted in Schore, 2001).

So what is happiness? Turning to the dictionary, I find definitions which explain both our attitude to happiness and perhaps some misconceptions. Each first designation mentions luck or fortune. The word derives from hap, to happen, to come about by chance. Thus the misconceptions: that there is nothing we can do to attain happiness; or that by accumulating goods and power we can trick fortune and build barriers against chance. We can respond to this from two angles. We can try to build a fortress against chance or we can train ourselves to bend flexibly with the winds of change. This is touched upon in one definition: "having the feeling of satisfaction with one's circumstances". For circumstances are out of our control: we cannot will ourselves to be happy all the time, nor can we avoid all suffering. Buddhist teachings offer a wise response to an understanding of the nature of chance and change, and practices to help us to live peaceably with impermanence, to evade added suffering and sorrow by transforming the way we relate to what "haps". Beyond happiness itself lies a *way* to wellbeing—acknowledging the process of self in context. Turning again to the Dalai Lama (1998), "genuine happiness is characterised by inner peace and arises in the context of our relationships with others." This would seem a reasonable place from which to begin.

While I shall be writing much about Buddhist thought for its exquisite resource of wisdom and its two thousand years of introspective study and practices of awareness, I too, following humbly in the footsteps of His Holiness, seek a secular approach based on universal rather than on religious principles. In the last few years the Dalai Lama has been speaking and writing increasingly of Buddhist ideas and practices in terms of what he calls "basic spirituality". This basic spirituality or "genuine dharma" entails the cultivation of fundamental qualities such as goodness, kindness, compassion, patience, tolerance and a sense of responsibility, along with a disciplined state of mind which may be translated into appropriate action. It does not entail becoming something called "a Buddhist". The term *dharma* has several meanings: *dharma* denotes phenomena, sometimes in terms of the smallest atoms, which should, however, always be thought of in terms of dynamic arisings or events, both subjective and objective, rather than as substantial things. *Dharma* also refers to teachings and to truth. Yet there is a definite link between them. *Dharma*, the teachings, describes the way things ultimately occur; *dharma*, phenomena, physical and mental events, are the very building blocks of the way reality comes about. Thus to understand the Buddha's teaching is to see *Dharma*, the truth of things in terms of *dharmas*, impermanent yet dynamic and interconnected mental and physical events. But more about that later.

Back to wellbeing. Surely all of us in search of wellbeing can sign up to compassion and contentment? That sounds easy. But read on: it calls for nothing less than "a radical revolution away from our habitual preoccupation with self" (Dalai Lama, 1998). Can we in this Western era of ever-increasing consumption in support of ever more individualistic selves agree to this? It comes down to understanding where our wellbeing lies.

There can be no doubt that over the last century in the United States and in Europe life has become far easier and the majority of the population far wealthier in material terms. We enjoy comfort and choice never known before. Diseases that caused early death are now commonly cured. Death in childbirth is now relatively rare. Our families are mostly the size we choose them to be. If the weather is dire and the harvest poor, we no longer starve. Technological advances offer most of us an infinitely easier life. To return to old ways would entail unbearable drudgery. We expect time for leisure, and in that leisure we expect to be entertained, not to have to amuse ourselves. Our houses, even modest ones, contain material goods unimaginable a hundred years ago. But are we happier? It hardly seems so. Economic growth and prosperity have not been accompanied by increase in happiness. Many people still feel trapped. We hear a familiar litany, especially in the wealthier areas, of housing being unaffordable, of the need for two jobs to maintain the "necessary" lifestyle. We see children filling the hours with school and after-school activities in order to be able to take their places on the upward escalator. Is it staircase or treadmill? Time has now become the new luxury.

As the public, so our private lives are often also fragmented and alienated. We suffer stress, lack of time, lack of companionship, and lack of deep belief. It is a time of paradoxes. Greater prosperity leads to greater fear of losing what we have; greater choice leads to less direction, less purpose, more confusion. All around us we see the suffering of the seemingly privileged. We see that emotion is easily elicited by image, but that direct response to reality is avoided. We see acceptance of violence on screen but only lip service paid to rejecting it in life. An almost frantic search for an acceptable morality goes hand in hand with loss of all previous foundations for one. The fashionable, who stand as models for us ordinary beings as the gods once stood on Olympus, search for ever-wilder sensation and freedom. While ordinary mortals envy the stars, the stars complain of loss of privacy and defend their daily lives with bodyguards and high walls, prisoners of their own popularity.

Perhaps one relevant fact is that this very technologized age has left us unhinged, alienated from the context which makes our stories meaningful. In subtle ways we have become divorced from our embodiment, emotion, environment and creativity. Our comfort has cut us off from our environment, from awareness of our place in the world, from our embodied experience of it, and also, strangely, from other humans. We are an ever more rootless society, moving frequently away from family, tribe or clan into shifting patterns of transient, often shallow acquaintance. Families are smaller, generally unsupported by a network of extended relations. At the same time much more is expected from partnership. The partner is desired and expected to be lover, friend and parent. When partnerships crack under the strain of providing all this, divorce rates rise and children suffer. It is rarely pointed out that never before has so much been expected of partnerships, or indeed of self. Rather than the neuroses and psychoses of sexual repression described in Freud's case histories, today issues of self, of relationship and of meaning, depression, alienation and stress are the forms of anguish that most commonly bring people into the psychotherapists' offices.

Changes in contemporary life have made us strangely detached from our ongoing experience. Living almost exclusively within the human arena, seeing ourselves as controllers of the world, we have repressed our belonging to it. Other species are there as resources or as pets. They are no longer "others" of interest in their own right. The world itself is there as a resource to be used and profited from rather than as an active subject from which we can learn, which can surprise us, to which we belong. Thus we are shocked by hurricane, tsunami and flood. Our response is that it shouldn't really be like this. Surely the world is there for man?

On Sunday 9th March 2003 in the United Kingdom, the *Independent on Sunday* newspaper printed a whole-page article entitled "Don't worry, be happy (and pay your taxes)". It was subtitled "We make more money, but we're more depressed than ever. What's gone wrong?"[2] The article begins: "Here's a shocking fact. Despite our huge increases in affluence, people in the West have grown no happier in the past fifty years." In the same weekend, the *Financial Times* weekend issue devoted two whole pages to an article by Richard Tompkins, Business Journalist of the Year, entitled "How to be Happy" (8 March 2003). He too described how our transition to a society based on surfeit rather than scarcity is proving troublesome; how increased levels of prosperity have failed to deliver corresponding improvements in our sense of wellbeing. Both articles criticised conventional indices of progress, suggesting that new measurements of life satisfaction need to be added to the bare indices of economic growth. Layard suggested that such facts as those above "should make us rethink everything—our work-life balance, our attitudes to tax, our priorities for health, our whole moral philosophy" (2005, p. 23). Happiness, it would seem, is "moving up the political and cultural agenda". While this has yet to occur, the message is certainly spreading. By the middle of 2006, a major bookshop in London proudly displayed in its psychology department a table of several dozen recently published books under the headline "The Art of Happiness". Newspaper articles and television schedules are packed with the topic of happiness and its shadow side of depression. Everyone now knows about the example of Bhutan, the last independent Buddhist kingdom in the Himalayas, which has as one of its major political aspirations Gross National Happiness rather than Gross National Profit. The understanding is growing that if amelioration of outer circumstances fails to bring about a sense of wellbeing, we must turn inwards; the barriers to happiness now seem to be inner ones. Yet the idea that happiness and benevolent states of mind can be cultivated with practice is a radical one from our normal Western perspective.

The ancient Greeks had a term *eudaimonia*—flourishing or wellbeing. In all sorts of ways and on all sorts of levels the human organism wishes to flourish. At the simplest level this concerns basic homeostasis, another Greek word signifying balance. On this most primary level occur simple responses concerned with survival, with finding, incorporating and transforming energy, with approach to and withdrawal from external objects, and with increase and decrease of activity. According to the model presented by the neuroscientist Antonio Damasio, further up the organisational ladder we find competitive and co-operative responses, drives and motivations, on up to emotions. As we shall consider in more detail later, he divides emotions into primary emotions, basic emotions such as anger, social emotions such as shame, and the consciousness of these emotions that he terms feelings (Damasio, 2003, pp. 46–49). In a neuroscientific reframing of the first and second ennobling truths of Buddhism, Damasio writes: "The yearning for homeostatic correctives would have begun as a corrective to anguish" (*ibid.*, p. 271). He recounts that the neurobiology of emotion and feeling shows that joy is preferable to sorrow, that it is more conducive to health and the "creative flourishing of our beings" (*ibid.*). Eudaimonia again. It is also affected by others. Damasio notes that "the very prospect of suffering and death breaks down the homeostatic process in the beholder" (*ibid.*, p. 270). This agrees well with the Dalai Lama's definition of happiness as being characterised by inner peace that arises in the context of a relationship with the other.

I wonder sometimes if our lack of happiness also reflects our current interpretation of what defines happiness. As consumers of our experience we want our happiness to be the best, the happiest and our own. Unsatisfied with mere contentment or equilibrium, we aspire to happiness as some continuous personal high, disconnected from inner peace and relationship. Another problem lies with our tendency to reify anything and everything, including happiness. Positive and negative vary with circumstance, and to cling to positive states may be enough to render them destructive. Happiness may be inappropriate in a sorrowful circumstance, and true wellbeing demands that we are able to cope appropriately with times of inevitable suffering, our own or that of others. Happiness may become just another goal to achieve, with consequent guilt and shame if not realized. Natural happiness may be a little different from our current aspirations for it. Our very unconscious processes strive towards homeostasis, survival with a sense of wellbeing. We could say that some form of the search for flourishing is inbuilt and unconscious, wired into our bodies. Could we say that our Buddha nature is truly embodied?

Today neuroscientists are exploring these areas. They have findings of tremendous importance to tell us: findings that could and should alter our daily lives, our search for happiness. In earlier times it was the province of religion and philosophy to teach us how best to live. Recently these disciplines have been to some extent undermined by the discoveries of science, which have either contradicted or made irrelevant their truths. Perhaps the time is right for a new, different conversation between science and spirituality or "basic Dharma".

A few years ago a radical Christian theologian, Don Cupitt, suggested, rather as the Dalai Lama has done, that religion today should be viewed less as providing eternal truth than as a guide to living, as providing a set of spiritual tools for enhancing our lives in a manner similar to that of art. He suggested that it might be "an experiment in selfhood".[3] Perhaps we can turn back to Buddhism with its long history of psychology to provide us with an *experiment in non-selfhood*? Such an experiment may enable that "radical revolution away from our habitual preoccupation with self" that may lead us to wellbeing. A dialogue would seem to be coming into focus between these basic forms of spirituality, the new findings of neuroscience and the experience of psychotherapy, based on new understandings of what it means to be human, taking into consideration the view from within and without, both the first and the third person perspectives.

Psychotherapy is the discipline most concerned with individual happiness and its lack. Recently psychotherapy has frequently usurped, or by default fallen into, a quasi-religious role of reconciling us to our lives. Sometimes this is helpful, but I suggest that psychotherapy generally lacks a philosophical or an ethical basis that can enable therapists to grapple with the fundamental questions of what they are doing and why. What is wellbeing? What is a healthy relationship between individual and world? In the absence of such thought there is a danger that some psychotherapeutic solutions offer mere sticking plaster: that, as with so much of contemporary allopathic medicine, they deal well with symptoms but suffer from a lack of concern with the whole. Moreover, there is a cogent argument that much of psychotherapy, with its over-emphasis on the individual and the inner, on the private perspective of the isolated individual, has often exacerbated the very alienation that brought many into therapy in the first place. Rather than reconciling the individual to the world and to society, such psychotherapy has focused only on individuality and uniqueness and the *right* to happiness. The separate story is emphasized at the expense of the greater picture, and often blame is evoked rather than compassion. Such psychotherapy may have encouraged the "me" society, ever more alienated from what is other, what is not me. It has furthered a retreat from society, from political action, into an ever more egocentric world. And the shadow of egocentricity is emptiness and lack. If hysteria as a result of sexual repression was the chief presenting problem of Freud's patients, today narcissism may be the neurosis of the age. Issues of self, of meaning and esteem, and the breakdown of fragile relationships which are asked to provide an impossible support for the empty self are the daily bread of the psychotherapist's office. Narcissism has twin poles of grandiosity and emptiness. A puffing up, an inflation of image, through fantasy or through consumption, covers feelings of loss, emptiness and lack of self-esteem. Narcissists use dominance to cover up dependence. Our alienation from the rest of the world, our isolated individuality, disallows us from admitting and receiving our true connection and interdependence.

Whilst one might have thought that psychology and psychotherapy were to some extent partners, the latter the experimental foundation for the practices of the former, this has not always been the case. Indeed, some years back, in the early days of writing my doctoral thesis on Buddhist philosophy and psychology as an inspiration for a contemporary psychotherapy, I dutifully began by defining my terms. Psychology, I wrote, is the science of the nature, function and phenomenon of the human soul or mind, as it is defined in the Oxford Dictionary. *Psychotherapy*, I stated, is the practice of treating psychic dis-ease founded upon the findings of psychology. My advisor, a psychologist, quickly pointed out that this was actually far from the case. The two disciplines had largely followed separate paths that rarely crossed, and had over the years communicated surprisingly little. Soon after Sigmund Freud first published his writings, academic psychology banished the study of subjective states of mind from its researches until well after the middle of the twentieth century. During these years the controlling scientific paradigm accepted only the study of visible behaviours. John B. Watson, a pre-eminent professor of psychology at Johns Hopkins University, wrote in 1914: "It is possible to write a psychology ... and never to use the terms consciousness, mental states, mind, content, will, imagery and the like" (1925, p. 9). For many decades after this, the pioneering experientially-based writings of William James were ignored, as consciousness and mind were pushed out beyond the boundaries of a "scientific" psychology. Only testable behaviours, stimulus and response were considered fit for study and research.

Ironically, it was only when studies into artificial intelligence entailed studies of hidden and "mental" processes that this most seemingly obvious lack was addressed. It was not until the second half of the twentieth century that the so-called cognitive revolution began, and consideration of conscious experience re-entered the field of academic psychology. Since then this field of the mind sciences has become one of the vital and exciting areas of contemporary science. This has been facilitated by a transformation in science itself. Theories of complexity, chaos and dynamic systems present a new vision of causality which states that a consequence arises from networks of multiple and reciprocal causes rather than from linear causality, thus allowing for the complexity of feedback loops and both upward and downward causation. This has had a decisive influence on contemporary science, affecting all its domains, but perhaps particularly those of the human and social sciences. In the realm of the mind sciences it has brought together a new collaboration of specialists, psychologists, neuroscientists, immunologists, neuropsychologists, linguists and even philosophers within a discipline which goes under several names: mind science, cognitive science, neuroscience (affective, cognitive, and even contemplative), and consciousness studies.

While some in this field still hold to an early guiding metaphor of brain as computer and mind as software, many are holding much more complex and open views and are eagerly grasping new technological innovations such as fMRI (functional magnetic resonance imaging) and the latest EEC (electroencephalogram) to explore the messier business of relating neural activity to subjective feel. For the so-called "hard problem", the problem of consciousness, is still just that—a problem. While most in the field are physicalists, believing that mind is, at base, part of the brain, the actual relationship is still unexplained. At the far materialist end of the spectrum are reductive physicalists; at the other end are substance dualists and the wonderfully titled "mysterians" who believe in an unfindable non-physical soul. Or at least they believe the problem is one that will never be solved, being outside the capacity of our mental equipment to solve it. Between these poles there are many positions, non-reductive physicalists, epiphenomenalists and others, which I will look at in more detail later.[4] The precise positions are less significant than the fact that the jury is still out. To date there is no general consensus. The "gap" remains between neuroscientific readings of neuronal activity in the brain and chemical activity in the body, and our subjective "feel" of things. It is an exciting time in the mind sciences, and a good time to bring such studies into the long-running conversation between psychotherapy and Buddhism's "first" psychology. Such a conversation may now be based on new understandings of what it means to be human, bringing together the view from within and without, both the first and the third person perspectives.

What is becoming increasingly clear is that many of our fundamental beliefs about ourselves, the certainties of earlier philosophy and our common sense folk psychology, are false. Our minds and bodies are not separate; we are through and through embodied creatures. Our reason and emotions are not separate; they too are through and through interconnected. Much of what we have always considered to be most human about ourselves and most conscious is found to happen quite happily below the level of consciousness. Nor can individuals be usefully considered in isolation from their environment, whether physical or cultural. Most exciting perhaps is the long overdue acknowledgement of neuroplasticity, the notion that the brain continually changes in response to our experiences, both through forming new connections between neurons and through the generation of new neurons. Whilst much of what we consider most nearly our selves is determined and largely occurs beyond the reach of consciousness or control, there are actions we can take and practices we can engage in which can influence our development either for better or for worse. Such new knowledge requires action, but science is rarely concerned with individual action and daily practice, nor have we yet accustomed ourselves to the idea that happiness and wellbeing are skills that may be cultivated by wise training.

For over two thousand years Buddhism has provided practices and a path towards readjusting our natural beliefs in a manner that would lead most surely to mental wellbeing. Practices are what we need now, practices which help us to cultivate happiness and teach restraint of that which promotes anguish. A dialogue has grown up over the past century between Buddhism and psychotherapy. The time is now right to expand this conversation, weaving together the new hard scientific evidence from the field of consciousness studies with the practical introspective experience of Buddhism, and contemporary psychotherapy, all in the context of our experience and in the service of the search for wellbeing.

Notes

1.   Reinhold Niebuhr wrote this prayer, although it is often incorrectly attributed to Saint Francis.
2.   Richard Layard, *Independent on Sunday* 9 March, 2003. Lord Layard is co-director of the Centre of Economic Performance at the London School of Economics. In the previous week he had presented three lectures on happiness as part of a series which has since been expanded and published in book form (Layard, 2005). Under the guidance of Lord Layard, in June 2006 the London School of Economics brought out a paper regarding the ubiquity of depression and its cost to the British nation, supporting an increase in psychotherapeutic provision in the National Health Service.
3.   From an interview in *The Guardian* newspaper, 10 February 1997.
4.   See van Gulick (2001).

CHAPTER TWO

The contemporary explanation: the mind sciences

I believe the new knowledge may change the human playing field.

(Damasio, 2003, p. 289)

Reality is under constant review.

(Broks, 2003, p. 20)

The more you learn about how the brain actually works, the more magical the apparatus seems. The more you learn about the brain, the more you understand how exquisitely crafted it is to record the unique contours of your own life in the unthinkably interconnected neurons and their firing patterns.

(Johnson, 2004)

The world is not a predetermined given set of facts; we construct the world with our observations.

(Turrell, 1996)[1]

New contemporary explanations of how our minds work are coming in almost daily from the broad field of the mind sciences. Mind, consciousness and experience have been "rediscovered" by science, and have become not only a permissible but also an exciting and "hot" domain for discovery. Indeed, the 1990s were described as the "decade of the brain". Earlier, despite experiential beginnings in the work of German introspectionists such as Wilhelm Wundt and the work of William James in the USA, the young field of psychology had turned away from the study of conscious subjective experience. The desire to be considered a bona fide science and to be consistent with the rigours of scientific method that called for objectivity, repeatability and verifiability restricted the acceptable field of research to consideration of visible and testable behaviours. Not until the end of the 1950s, and ironically through progress in work with artificial intelligence, did what came to be called "the cognitive revolution" begin. Only then were mind, experience and consciousness welcomed back into the scientific arena.

Thus a new interdisciplinary field opened up. Psychologists, linguists, neurologists, ethologists, computer scientists and even philosophers began to study mental actions such as memory, feeling and knowing, and a new field known as cognitive science came into being. In 1960 a landmark occurred with the founding of Harvard University's interdisciplinary Center for Cognitive Studies by Jerome Bruner and George Miller. Interestingly, by 1990 Bruner, one of the fathers of the cognitive revolution, was disenchanted with his child, believing that cognitive studies, rather than bringing mind and meaning back into the human sciences "after a long cold winter of objectivism", had been technicalized "in a manner that betrayed its original impulse" (Bruner, 1990, p. 126). Some years on, while Bruner would hopefully be gratified by some if not all of the multifarious happenings in the field, technologization, objectification and resistance to experience still remain, and there is some way to go for the fully humanized science that Bruner longed for. As late as 1989, the following definition appeared in the International Dictionary of Psychology: "Consciousness is a fascinating but elusive phenomenon. It is impossible to specify what it is, what it does or why it evolved. Nothing worth reading has been written about it" (Lodge, 2002, p. 6, quoting S. Sutherland). Agreeing with the lack of specification, but with a more hopeful attitude, in 1998 the philosopher John Searle wrote that as recently as 20 years previously, questions about consciousness had not been regarded as respectable scientific questions, and suggested that as far as definitions go, we were at the common sense description stage rather than an analytic stage. He gave his common sense definition of consciousness as consisting of "those states of sentience, or feeling, or awareness, which begin in the morning when we awake from a dreamless sleep and continue throughout the day until we fall into a coma, or die, or fall asleep again, or otherwise become unconscious" (Searle, 1998, p. 718). (By this definition dreams are a form of consciousness, although of course they are qualitatively different and have quite different characteristics from ordinary waking consciousness.)

The cognitive revolution has been accompanied by another upheaval in science which has also supported research into consciousness and experience. This is the rise of dynamic systems theory and complexity theory, which has had a profound impact on the framework of recent science. While classical science explained closed systems and the physical behaviour of mechanical objects, this new science has arisen from attempts to understand dynamic, open and complex systems such as weather, ecosystems and the experience of living beings. This radical reframing comes largely from a new vision of causality wherein a consequence is seen to arise from networks of multiple causes rather than from a single direct cause. Complex systems such as brain function develop emergent properties, properties generated by interactions within the system as a whole rather than by the actions of any single part. These emergent properties are more than the sum of their parts. At high levels of complexity they also demonstrate their own causal power, producing top-down changes to lower levels of the system. Thus we find two-way causation, both bottom-up and top-down.

This notion of non-linear or emergent dynamics replacing the earlier mechanistic paradigm has stimulated the re-examination of many models and encouraged new approaches to old problems such as the relations between the biological and the mental, the physical and the lived, the personal and the social. Some of the major features of this new approach are a concern with emergent properties, self-regulation, and feedback loops that allow for both upward and downward causation. Non-linear dynamic network models replace linear hierarchical ones; context and complexity replace isolated events and reductivity; process is emphasised rather than matter; and subjectivity and experience join objectivity as valid objects of study. Such an approach allows multifaceted processes to be explored in all their complexity. Let's take for example, the experience of stress. Overwork, worry and pressure, all social structures, produce stress, which generates somatic symptoms, high blood pressure, racing pulse, maybe panic attacks and so forth. These in turn have an effect on mood, causing fear and increasing stress that again affects our immune system. So a vicious cycle of interlocked processes ensues. Similarly, we can use dynamic models to consider other processes such as depression, where social, psychological and physiological factors interact in ever-widening feedback loops. On the larger scale of weather systems, the so-called "butterfly effect" points to the way a minor factor—the flight of a butterfly in one location—may eventually, after many interrelated causes and conditions, cause a major weather event many thousands of miles away.

In what was once the domain of psychology representatives of many disciplines now work together, and we find many different designations: cognitive science, neuroscience (both affective and cognitive, and even most recently social and contemplative), neuropsychology, neurophilosophy, neurobiology, behavioural neurology and consciousness studies, not to mention neuroethics. One of the important figures in this field, the neuroscientist Michael Gazzaniga, has suggested the name of Mind Sciences for the field, speaking of the "death of psychology" and stating that

> Psychology as a term has been hijacked by the clinicians and counsellors and has little relationship to the activities of academic psychologists and other mind scientists. That is fine. What is done now by people who study the mind is a vast array of activities that range from evolutionary theory to psychophysics, neuroscience, economics, anthropology and computer science, to mention a few. [1998, p. 711]

Within this broad field, there are so many approaches and variations in description that, as a non-scientist, I attempt a short overall guiding map of the field with immense trepidation. What has become known as the "hard problem", the explanatory gap between subjective experience and neuronal-level explanation is central to discussion and disputes in the domain. This is the problem of the gap between external scientific descriptions of neurological activity and the internal "feel" of what is happening for the experiencer. Think of it. Every action, every thought, every feeling occurs in at least two modalities. There is the action that occurs, probably unconsciously in the body-mind network, where many transactions are occurring at the neurological level. Chemical and electrical messages are sent and received, resulting in action, or feeling or thought. While these transactions may now be picked up by the new generation of tremendously sophisticated instruments such as fMRI (functional magnetic resonance imaging) and PET (positron emission tomography) scans, at the other level, the concurrent private, subjective *feelings* of these, often given the term "qualia", are both invisible and, so far, objectively indescribable. Thus whilst neuroscientists are busy working out how brain processes occur, their research is giving rise to wider philosophical issues: fundamental questions concerning consciousness, selves, and our experience of others—theory of mind and empathy.[2] While some scientists believe that it is only a matter of time before science will reveal the answers to these conundrums, others consider it unlikely that neuroscience alone can solve such problems and that they require a more philosophical approach. Thus both scientific and philosophical enquiries are found in the extensive field of the mind sciences.

With caution then, let us attempt to look at the diversity of opinion in the field. There is broad agreement on a physicalist stance. The old Cartesian dualism of mind and matter is over, despite our popular and daily and unconscious enacting of it. However, beyond this agreement huge differences are to be found. On the near side of the field are the physical reductionists for whom mind and brain overlap completely. For these extreme reductionists consciousness is reduced to neural mechanisms alone.

A second, and probably the largest grouping is that of the "functionalists", less reductive physicalists who are centrally concerned with the importance of systems and their interrelations. They hold that mental states, rather than being completely identical with brain states, are defined by their functional organization, the patterns of causal relations within the neuronal networks. Unlike the neoreductionists, functionalists pay attention to nonlinear neural patterns, but they deny that consciousness is an emergent phenomenon, one that is irreducible to its parts. Rather, many consider that consciousness is an epiphenomenon, a process which arises out of and is inseparable from brain processes but which lacks causal power of its own.

A further grouping comes under the delightful name of Mysterians. They believe that the problem of consciousness is ultimately unsolvable. This name embraces both substance dualists who believe in a substance beyond the reach of science like the old "mind", and those, less extreme, who merely believe that we are too implicated within consciousness to gain a perspective on it, just as an eye cannot see itself. Yet others seek an explanation for consciousness in quantum processes which are as yet not entirely understood.

It is with the radical and somewhat maverick Enactive approach that I wish to engage most fully. While there are differences of position within this grouping, in general they have followed the implications of earlier systems research which considered human beings as open systems influenced by environment and relationship, and then concluded that this requires a complete upheaval of approach both methodologically and philosophically. Traditional notions of representation and computation, they believe, are inadequate to understand the complex interactions of brain, body and world. Enactive cognitive scientists believe, on the evidence of present research, that progress in understanding will require both the new tools and methods of nonlinear dynamic systems theory and also an understanding that the processes critical for consciousness cut across our conventional brain-body-world divisions; they cannot adequately be represented as brain-bound neural events. Thus they turn to science, to phenomenological philosophy and to Eastern forms of meditation to find tools to explore experience from both objective and subjective poles and close the explanatory gap between neuronal and experiential levels. In an appendix I will describe the enactive viewpoint from the description of one of its originators, but here I would like to turn to the major findings to date of what has sometimes been called the "second generation" of mind scientists.

Beyond all these divisions, what is most exciting and important to me about these new mind sciences is not history or name or organisation but the implications of the research. New discoveries are arising from this field that may change our understanding of the ways we think and act. New techniques of brain scanning enable scientists to create visual maps of the brain which can show difference according to what is being experienced. Likewise the location of biochemicals and their receptors have also been mapped. These are discoveries concerning the way our minds and bodies work which can really help us live healthily and happily. Finally, psychology and psychotherapy can come together. The theoretical field, call it psychology, mind science, cognitive science or neuroscience, has messages of importance for the practical and experiential field. Psychotherapists, counsellors, educators and those wishing to live happily should listen in. From the Buddhist perspective it is fascinating to see how these discoveries resonate with Buddhist philosophy, and how Buddhist practices may provide a resource for Western science. Some major trends may be encapsulated, obviously simplified, under three or four major headings which are in fact all interrelated. Each of these will be explored more fully in coming chapters.

Embodiment

For the past few centuries, after the Cartesian separation of mind and body, body has been undervalued in favour of mind, but recent research reveals that mind only exists in an embodied state. Indeed, much research points to the way that mind is not restricted to brain function. Mind processes are distributed throughout the body. As Candace Pert says, "Every change in physiological state is accompanied by an appropriate change in the mental emotional state, conscious or unconscious; conversely every change in the mental emotional state, conscious or unconscious, is accompanied by an appropriate change in the physiological state" (1997, p. 137). Thus the division of body and mind is literally unthinkable. Which leads to:

Emotion

As body was disregarded in favour of mind, so emotion has long been disregarded in favour of cognition and rationality. Emotion, inextricably bound to our embodiment, as we saw above, is now seen to play an integral part in all cognition and experience. It is at the very foundation of our daily interaction with the world. Our sensing of the exterior world is filtered along sensory pathways and way-stations, each of which has emotional tone. What we perceive as real is filtered through a gradient of past emotions and learning.

Emotion is now seen as the mechanism that enables the organism to adapt physiologically, psychologically and behaviourally in response to environmental challenges. As Pert says, "Emotions are constantly regulating what we experience as 'reality'. The decisions about what sensory information travels to your brain and what gets filtered out depends on what signals the receptors in your cells are receiving from peptides" (ibid., p. 147). Peptides are the chemicals that bind to the neuroreceptors in cells, conveying messages throughout the body. These two, receptors and ligands (the substances that bind to the receptors), are what Pert has named the molecules of emotion.

Emotions are seen to have played an important evolutionary role in helping us decide what is worth paying attention to and what to ignore. Closely linked as they are to memory, emotions are also instrumental in deciding what we remember and what we forget. Far from being unimportant or something of a nuisance (and I would make a brief diversion here just to note how commonly emotion has been designated as particularly "feminine"), emotions are seen to be fundamental for all cognition and behaviour. Mediating between organism and world, discussion of emotion leads inevitably to discussion of:

Environment

This refers broadly to situatedness, our embedding in the world. As we have seen above, we are not context-independent but intricately interwoven with our context, our environment, both our physical environment and our cultural and social one. As the anthropologist Clifford Geertz wrote, "Brains and cultures have co-evolved, mutually dependent the one on the other for their very realization" (2000, p. 205).

Several features contribute to the importance of environment. One is ecology; another is culture—the influence of the mental landscape of custom, belief and even personal experience within which we live. Perhaps most fundamental is the important environment of intersubjectivity, our dependence upon others of our species. The discovery of mirror neurons in the premotor area of monkeys' brains has the potential for explaining the mimicking process central to human mind-reading, empathy, learning, and possibly even the evolution of language. Certain cells which are activated when a monkey performs a highly specific action with its hand, such as pulling, pushing or grasping, are also seen to fire when the monkey merely watches another monkey (or even the experimenter) perform the same action. The neuroscientist V. S. Ramachandran, who has carried out research into the existence of these neurons in the human brain, has suggested that this discovery will do for psychology what the discovery of DNA did for biology. Most telling, from my perspective, is the fact that he has nicknamed them "empathy" or (better still) "Dalai Lama" neurons, as they seemingly dissolve the barrier between self and other.[3] Mind sciences are revealing how profoundly our individual minds in their development are influenced, even to the extent of physiological formation, by our experience of interpersonal relationships and patterns of communication. Bringing together all these points of embodiment, emotion and environment, Geertz (2000) has written:

> Our brains are not in a vat, but in our bodies. Our minds are not in our bodies, but in the world. And as for the world, it is not in our brains, our bodies or our minds: they are, along with gods, verbs, rock and politics, in it.

Throughout all the topics above runs another theme, that of the *unconscious*. Maybe I should call it non-conscious. This is distinctly *not* the Freudian unconscious of repression, nor the Jungian collective unconscious reservoir of archetypes. This is just non-conscious, that which is naturally occurring below the level of consciousness. Non-conscious processes are seen to be central to our development, both physically and emotionally. Rationality and consciousness, it is being discovered, only come into being as the very icing on the cake of non-conscious processes. They rest on the largely unconscious affective responses of the body. Allan Schore, one of the leading figures in this research, has gone as far as to suggest (2004) that the implicit self system of the right brain which evolves in early preverbal development represents the biological instantiation of the psychoanalytic dynamic unconscious. However, while our attention is being unconsciously directed by the flow of chemicals in our bodies and we are not consciously involved in deciding what is attended to, we do have the possibility of bringing some of these decisions into consciousness and overriding what we might call our "default" process with the help of various kinds of attentional training. We are beginning to shed more light on this area which has always been the space of psychotherapy.

One of the most exciting finds is that of *neuroplasticity*. Both biochemical processes and physiological brain growth that influence our experience are themselves influenced by, and respond to, experience. One of the most important discoveries in the mind-body field is the fact that this is a two-way process. The brain develops in response to experience. Research shows that attentional patterns can physically alter the neural pathways in the brain.[4] This has enormous implications for our understanding of development, both healthy and pathological, and for methods of recovery. Professor Paul Bach-y-Rita of the University of Wisconsin has perhaps explored furthest in the realms of neuroplasticity.[5] Understanding that we see not with our eyes but with our brains, he has created methods for using surviving sensory systems such as skin and tongue to substitute for lost vision. He is currently patenting a device that uses electrical impulses to route special information through the tongue to the brain. This technology could be used to enable divers to "see" better in murky waters and soldiers to enhance their night vision. He is also working on flight suits embedded with transducers, mini vibrators like those found in mobile phones, to expand awareness and enhance "vision" for pilots whose normal sight organs are overloaded with the needs of their visual workloads.

Implications for Psychotherapy

All the topics above are brought together in current work within the field of development and attachment theory. Some half-century ago, John Bowlby, a British psychoanalyst, argued that developmental processes were best understood as the interaction of nature and nurture, of a unique genetic contribution and a particular environment. He created a body of research and theory which suggested that early patterns of attachment between infant and caregiver have a profound impact on social, emotional and intellectual growth. Today new research is giving this theory the neurological foundations it lacked, which led to its comparative disregard for so long. Bowlby's theory has now been synthesised with psychobiological and neurobiological research particularly in the work of Professor Allan Schore (1994, 2001, 2003, 2005) and his colleagues at UCLA, Daniel Siegel & Louis Cozolino (Siegel, 2001, 2007; Cozolino, 2002, 2006) which has brought together structural and functional explanations and demonstrated how schemas of attachment are instantiated into the brain.

Human infants are not born with all their capacities; these develop over time. Since such development takes place outside the womb, it is open to influence from the environment.[6] Research clearly shows the importance of relationship in this development, not only for behaviour but also for actual physiological growth: brain structure and chemistry develop in response to experience. Confirming the centrality of emotion, research is showing that in infancy and later, the regulation of emotion is central to human development and motivation, and this experience is embedded in the attachment relationship (Schore, 2001). In early infancy the relationship with the primary caregiver (usually the mother), starting with mutual gaze, is the primary mechanism for stimulating the growth and organization of the brain. Such physical and emotional engagement produces a cascade of biochemical processes that stimulate the growth and connectivity of neural networks. As Schore says, the maturation of the infant's brain is experience-dependent, and these experiences are embedded in the attachment relationship (1994, 2001). Research carried out with Romanian orphans has shown that those poor children who were deprived of loving and responsive contact, left in their cots all day, suffered not only mentally but also physiologically, having a "virtual black hole" where their orbitofrontal cortex should be (Gerhardt, 2004, p. 38; Chugani et al., 2001).

In descriptions of mother-baby interaction, many theoreticians have used the concept of "resonance", and write of unconscious right brain to right brain communication. Under healthy circumstances, mothers and their babies engage in attachment scenarios of "affective synchrony" whereby the good-enough caregiver, who is in sympathy with the baby's physical and psychological needs, regulates the baby's states of positive and negative affect. Such external regulation fosters the baby's developing capacity for self-regulation, the ability to tolerate and regulate stressful emotional states, and also the ability to experience interactive positive states of play and joy. It is only possible to learn self-management and develop capabilities of self-care and awareness of your own feeling if someone else has done it for you first. The baby needs a caregiver who can validate and make sense of their experience by responding accurately to what is actually happening in the present moment and reacting appropriately to their needs. The emotional experience of a baby becomes physiologically embedded. From the later stages in the womb through the first two years of life there is a growth phase in the right hemisphere of the brain, which is particularly concerned with emotional processing. Under normal conditions early mother-baby interactions facilitate the development of self-regulatory structures located in the cortico-limbic area of the right hemisphere of the brain. Positive emotional experience in this period gives rise to brains with richer neuronal connections; negative experience results in alterations in the biochemistry of the immature brain, which lead to altered right brain development and subsequent difficulty in emotional regulation. In later life, the individual's capacity to assimilate novel (and therefore potentially stressful) emotional experience will be compromised. Early relationships which convey an acceptance of the full range of feelings, both positive and negative ones, allow for such feelings to be fully experienced and tolerated in adult life.

If such relationships are not experienced, the free flow of feelings which is essential for mental and physical health is cut off. Profound disruption to this attachment bonding process, such as maternal deprivation or trauma, can produce psychobiological and neurochemical dysregulation in the developing brain and abnormal development of neurons, synapses and neurochemical processes. Stress hormones, aroused by negative experience such as the lack of suitable response to emotional arousal, prevent other positive biochemical processes which facilitate natural maturation. Dysfunctional development of emotional regulation may result in damage to the development of neuronal networks and biochemical functions as well as to psychological outlook, leaving permanent damage to both physiology and functioning, in particular an inability to regulate high stress states. Research has shown links between early developmental trauma and deficient response to stress and novelty. In normal development, the mother will not always respond in a symmetrical manner, that is to say a desired way from the baby's point of view. However, if experiences of asymmetry and disruption are followed by regulation and restoration of balance, they implicitly teach the baby that negative experience and novelty may be tolerated, thus instantiating resilience in the face of unpredictable experience. Such resilience will not be acquired by the infant experiencing traumatic or consistently asymmetrical and dysregulated maternal response. Such experience may create a later vulnerability to post-traumatic stress disorder (PTSD), depression, anxiety, addiction, eating disorders and also immune system injury (Schore, 2002, pp. 9–50). While early childhood is the most critical time, development need not end with childhood. Neuroplasticity continues throughout life. Just as early negative emotional experience can predispose a child to future emotional problems by creating distorted pathways, so care and attention in later life can attempt repair. In the absence of the growth spurts of early infanthood, however, this will take far greater time and effort. In a fascinating book Laura Sewell, a scientist concerned with the psychology of vision, suggests that even in adulthood specific activity and experience can materially continue to alter and develop our capacity for sight (1999). She reports that research into vision indicates that activation of attentional mechanisms is necessary for structural change to alter the visual cortex. Structural changes entail essential alterations in the strength of the synaptic connections between neurons, causing the formation of new neural associations and new pathways. Such synaptic connections are strengthened by usage, most significantly in conjunction with the presence of neurotransmitters subserving attentional mechanisms. Once strengthened, a synapse will require a lower threshold of input in order to fire or pass a message down its neural pathway. Such strengthening will then facilitate the activation of those neural networks. Such networks constitute our schemata, the way we readily categorize visual input; in short they determine our perceptual tendencies. So by strengthening certain synapses and particular neural pathways, our attentional choice may not only select and enhance specific information but also influence the way we categorize visual input. As we have seen, this occurs both healthily and unhealthily. In a non-visual example of neuroplasticity, the brains of violinists show greater cortical development in areas concerned with the fingers of the left hand than is found in the brains of non-string instrument players (Cozolino, 2002, p. 297; Elbert et al., 1995).

This has important implications for psychotherapy and for health. Understanding of both healthy and maladaptive emotional development gives us important clues as to methods of later repair, which I will outline in the next chapter. Once again research emphasises the importance of attention and awareness and of the cultivation of these processes. Meditation and mindfulness may provide such practices for a culture which has heretofore ignored emotional or attentional education in favour of the collection of facts. Candace Pert also points to a further benefit of meditation: she describes the mind-body network being overtaxed by unprocessed sensory input in the form of suppressed trauma or undigested emotions. Under such conditions the peptides cease to flow freely, and the largely automatic body-mind processes regulated by them suffer and cease to work smoothly. She recommends meditation as a way of allowing buried thoughts and emotions to resurface, thus reinstating the free flow of peptides and their important messages. Free and flexible flow of emotions is necessary for mental and physical health. When healthy emotional life is in flow, without blockages, feelings may come and go, being processed as they arise. Such flow, as we have seen, is not merely intrapersonal but also interpersonal.

This is a good moment to turn to Buddhism. We will consider in greater detail later how Buddhist theories of the way selves form resonate with these scientific findings. Although early Buddhists would not have expected this to occur in the form of chemical transmission, Buddhist models of the self describe how our attention and our perception are informed by our dispositions, which in their turn were formed by earlier perceptions and felt responses. We can also see how Buddhist practices of awareness and mind training provide an enormous resource for transforming mind and body.

As Western scientists concern themselves with the study of consciousness after decades when only visible behaviours were considered suitable subjects for scientific study, they are brought to a halt by the "hard problem" of the explanatory gap between descriptions on the level of neuronal activity and the experiential "feel" of the experience. As the patient lies in the scanner feeling darkness, perhaps fear, the touch of metal, and maybe both physical and psychological irritation, the watching scientist sees only patterns on the screen. In order to explore this first person subjective perspective to accompany the third person objective stance of Western science, some scientists studying consciousness, as we have noted, are approaching meditators. For experienced meditators have practised control of their mental processes which is far beyond the ordinary, to the extent that they are able to focus on specific mental processes at will.

At an Oxford symposium of the Enactive Consciousness Section of the British Psychological Society in the summer of 2003, there were several papers that referred directly to Buddhist ideas and practices. At the present time research is ongoing with experienced meditators as a result of the Mind and Life Conferences that have brought together leading Western scientists and the Dalai Lama.[7] Two of the most recent of these resulted in the written records *Destructive Emotions*, narrated by Daniel Goleman (2003), and *Visions of Compassion*, edited by Richard Davidson and Ann Harrington (2001). Since then Davidson, whose work has been in the field of neuroplasticity, the capacity of people to transform their emotion, behaviour, brain function and even brain conformation, has led the Madison Project. He has invited highly competent and experienced meditators into his laboratory to collaborate in brain imaging studies. He wishes to understand better what he terms altered states of consciousness, transformations of the brain and personality that both endure and foster wellbeing. Years earlier, while still at Harvard in the 1970s, Goleman and Davidson had co-authored an article which argued that training attention through meditation would create lasting and beneficial psychobiological changes. Only now does science have the tools to actually monitor this. Early results are interesting.[8] Initial work certainly suggests that meditation changes brain function. Today Davidson says: "In the scientific community, attention span and emotional regulation have been regarded as static abilities which can't be improved upon. The dialogue between science and Buddhism is helping to reframe our understanding of those processes as skills that can be trained."[9] Other studies have shown positive effects of meditation for a variety of health-related issues.[10] Perhaps most interesting from the perspective of our search for wellbeing, experiments at Madison studying the link between activity in the brain and states of meditative bliss have shown enormous increases in electrical activity in the left prefrontal lobe of the brain of an experienced meditator, demonstrating that happiness is not just some vague and indescribable feeling but also a physical state of the brain, and one that can be deliberately induced. Furthermore, such states have a powerful influence on our health. In a variety of experiments, those who rate highest in psychological tests relating to happiness, optimism and curiosity have also been found to have higher immune system responses to stressors such as flu vaccines, and to have a better response to a variety of diseases such as diabetes, cardiovascular disease and respiratory ailments.[11]

Awareness is seen to be central to mental and physical health. Intentional awareness does make a difference, but it takes practice, like other skills. The idea that we can cultivate practices that enhance our happiness is not one common to our Western traditions. Buddhism is a rich resource for awareness practices that can both foster wellbeing and help repair dis-ease.

Notes

1. Artist James Turrell, quoted in G. Willens, *The Sensuous Lushness of Light*. Turrell and Minnaert, Kijkduin, exhibition catalogue, the Hague Centre for the Visual Arts, 1996, and repeated in James Turrell Deer Shelter, Yorkshire Sculpture Park, Albion and The Arts Fund, 2006.
2. In later chapters, some of these issues will be discussed. In particular, Chapter Eight will consider some theories concerning selves.
3. The initial research was carried out by G. Rizzolatti. For more information see Gallese et al. (2004) and Gallese & Goldman (1998); for V. S. Ramachandran, see www.ede.org/3rdculture/ramachandran06.
4. For example research by Hubel & Wiesel (1964) regarding the visual cortex in kittens and Meany et al. (1996) on changes due to infant care.
5. This information comes from "Emerging Concepts of Brain Function", a paper delivered in Paris in June 2004 on the occasion of a conference entitled "From Autopoesis to Neurophenomenology" in tribute to F. J. Varela. Further information about this paper is available at. www. comdig.de, and about Professor Bach-y-Rita at www.wicab.com.
6. Some believe that pre-birth development within the uterus is also affected by events and experience.
7. For a history of these meetings see Goleman, *Destructive Emotions*, p.385, and Appendix 2.
8. See chapter "The Lama in the Lab", in Goleman, *Destructive Emotions*.
9. "Meeting of the Minds". Article in *Tricycle*, Spring 2005, p. 50.
10. The work of Jon Kabat Zinn is particularly relevant here. He has for many years used meditative practices removed from their Buddhist context for the relief of stress, the management of chronic pain, and in the treatment of psoriasis. See "Healing Mind, Healing Body." *Tricycle*, Spring 2005, p. 52.
11. See "The Biology of Joy", in *Time* magazine, 17 January 2005. This special Mind and Body issue has several interesting articles relating to happiness.

CHAPTER THREE

Psychotherapy: explanation in action

The mind is its own place, and in itself
Can make a Heav'n of Hell, a Hell of Heav'n.

(Milton, *Paradise Lost*, l. 249)

Who going through the vale of misery, use it for a well and
the pools are filled with water.

(Psalm 5)

A brief history

P sychotherapy is the Western expression of a practical exploration of emotion. Daniel Goleman has referred to it as "emotional tutorial". Its particular expertise is in paying attention
to emotions which have been ignored, suppressed or repressed and
which lie beneath conscious awareness. As we have seen above, new
research shows this to be ever more important.

First of all, there are even more psychotherapies than there are
"Buddhisms". Moreover, unlike Buddhism, there is no central core
of teachings to which one can point as the heart of all psychotherapy.

Perhaps the central pivot may be said to be the intention: the treatment and alleviation of mental or physical distress through the careful consideration of mental processes. It is difficult today to imagine this without the work of Freud and his discoveries of the unconscious repression of emotionally upsetting material, and its liberation through the "talking cure". While many of his beliefs and working methods have been challenged, it is largely in response to his pioneering work that the many and various schools of psychotherapy have sprung into being, and even today, as we shall see, neuroscience is suggesting new interpretations of his theory. While I believe it is possible to give at least a cursory description of the field under the main headings of four different "umbrella" schools, more than ever one must be aware that the map is not the territory.

As stated, the first and pivotal school is that of psychoanalysis, starting with the work of Freud. For those of us who are not psychoanalysts, the tendency of those who are to commandeer the field and look down upon other practitioners is sometimes annoying, as is the tendency of laymen to think of psychoanalysts as the only psychotherapists. However, there is no avoiding the fact that psychoanalysis was historically the first significant school of psychotherapy, and it is the one against which almost all subsequent theories have defined themselves, in redescription or opposition.

Freud's theory of psychoanalysis, though it changed somewhat over the years, basically presented a dynamic theory of the interactions between conflicting forces in the mind which arise when instinctual drives confront external necessity. His first model of mind showed it as being divided into conscious, preconscious and unconscious regions. Later he described it structurally as having three agencies: *id*, which relates to instinctual drives, primarily that of libido or erotic drive (although Freud later added a death instinct, *thanatos*); *ego*, which is developed as a mediator between the drives and the exigencies of the world; and *superego*, which represents social and parental influences brought to bear upon the drives. His aim was encapsulated in the statement "Where id was, there shall ego be." However, his view of life was basically pessimistic, to replace uncontrolled neurosis with "ordinary neurosis", an acceptable level of accommodation with the drives. In his view unacceptable neurosis was caused by the inappropriate return of repressed material, such as repressed desires, in the form of symptoms. What he termed the repression of the "pleasure principle" in the service of the "reality principle" serves to keep unacceptable (by the standards of society) desires out of consciousness. Psychoanalysis is the process of retrieval of this repressed material through the interpretations of a skilled analyst and the "talking cure", using the technique of free association, which loosens the hold of the conscious rational mind that inhibits buried memories. Through uncovering the repressed causes of the neurosis, the patient is relieved of the conflict and the symptoms are dissolved.

Two important pillars of Freudian analysis are the Oedipus complex and transference. The Oedipus complex forms part of the Freudian model of psychosocial and psychosexual development through distinct stages. Healthy personal development depends on successful resolution and integration of these stages. The Oedipal experience arises for males in the phallic phase, where craving for the attention of mother and antagonism towards the father as rival gives rise to phantasies of the killing of the father and possession of the mother. This incestuous desire is abandoned in the face of the father's perceived threat of castration. A boy then moves from his love for his mother to identification with the father. The female path is more complex, and Freud's description of it, and his understanding of the feminine psyche, has generally been considered inadequate.[1] Transference is the way the analysand transfers onto the analyst the psychic conflicts that he may have experienced in the past. Awareness and use of this transference to uncover the hidden is a central tenet of psychoanalysis. Countertransference refers to the analyst's response to the analysand's transference. Traditional psychoanalysis was seen as a deep, long-term and frequent therapy. The relationship between analyst and analysand was in principle (though not always in practice) distant, the analyst's anonymity providing space for the analysand to project upon him historic themes.

There were many differences of opinion and interpretation within psychoanalysis, setting the trend for breakaway movements. Rank, Adler and Jung all fell out with Freud in what can only be seen as somewhat Oedipal conflicts. Since the time of Freud, even within psychoanalysis there have been many developments. Two main lineages followed different aspects of his work, that of the instincts and that of personal development. Ego psychology, following the lead of his daughter Anna, continued in a more traditional Freudian manner, but increasingly focusing on the development, function and strengthening of the ego. Elsewhere, development turned away from psychobiology towards developmental personality theory. The Object Relations school in England and Interpersonal Relations theory in the United States turned their attention away from concern with the biological or system ego and the maturation of instincts towards exploration of the ego's experience with objects of relationship, a perhaps unfortunate term for "others". In a far more intersubjective turn, carers and the environment are seen to play an important role in development: if the environment does not satisfy needs of supporting and understanding, development will be distorted or arrested. The proposition of libidinal and aggressive drives regulated by a developing ego is replaced by a psychosomatic whole developing its identity and characteristics through relationship.

As we saw in the last chapter, recent scientific research has re-activated and re-visioned this outlook, providing underlying neurological foundation for attachment theory and thereby providing a new outlook on some of Freud's theory. Many analysts have re-centred their work around this now scientifically validated attachment theory concerning the interaction of infant and mother[2] rather than on the more literary and metaphorical (and scientifically unproven) Oedipal theory. Continuing the embodiment of theory in the wake of recent scientific research, Allan Schore has suggested that "the emotion processing right mind is the neurobiological substrate of Freud's dynamic unconscious" (2003b, vol. 2). Recent discoveries of the ongoing neural plasticity of brain processes and continual right brain growth spurts along with the dyadic expansion of consciousness suggest that the dynamic unconscious may be to some extent repaired: in Schore's own words, "capable of becoming more complex as a result of effective, affectively-focused psychoanalytic treatment" (ibid.). As I stated earlier, psychotherapists of other persuasions would challenge the limitation of therapy to psychoanalysis. What may well be of import, however, is the understanding of the importance of affect and relationship in the therapeutic encounter.

The second major school of cognitive and behavioural psychotherapy is the one to date most linked with scientific and experimental psychology. Behavioural therapy originated as a reaction to the dominance of psychoanalysis. It began as an application of the principles of classical and operant conditioning to the treatment of problem behaviours. The theories on which it was founded, and with which academic psychology was at the time much concerned, stated that behaviour was the result of learning through conditioning and stimulus-response mechanisms. As described elsewhere, a cognitive revolution occurred in psychology which contended that intelligence lay not merely in stimulus and response and visible behaviour, but in an organism's ability to mentally represent aspects of the world and then to operate on such mental representations. Since then, cognition has been accepted as a major determinant of feelings and actions which can then be modified, thus effecting changes in behaviour through taking into account feelings, beliefs and expectations.

Cognitive behavioural psychotherapy consists of approaches that attempt to alleviate distress and dysfunction by identifying distortions in thinking, formulating alternative ways of viewing situations, and testing implications in action. Such therapies are usually more concerned with present experience than historical development. They tend to be shorter-term and more goal-specific than other therapies. Actual therapy is often concerned with step by step procedures: identifying problematic behaviours and beliefs, determining assets and resources which can be mobilised to motivate and maintain change, setting up treatment goals, and designing strategies to achieve these. The stance of the therapist is educative and directive. Since this form of therapy is usually relatively short-term and has distinct goals and measurable outcomes, it has recently become the favoured form of therapy within public and commercially funded organisations. A recent practice called Mindfulness Based Cognitive Therapy, bringing together mindfulness practices and cognitive therapy, has been proved to be of great use in treating depression.

The third, and probably the largest and most heterodox school of psychotherapy is the Humanistic school, under which I will also include the Existential approach, for the major distinction of this school from that of the psychoanalytic schools is the shift from the medical model and scientifically oriented perspective to the phenomenological, from concern with instincts to concern with individually experienced existence. Humanistic therapies also display a shift from the intrapsychic to the interpersonal and a holistic understanding of mind and body, and individual and world. Previous therapies come to be seen as too cognitive and technological at the expense of sensation and emotion. Therapeutic approaches are designed to correct dehumanisation, disembodiment and alienation.

Early existential psychotherapy was an attempt to bond a Freudian understanding onto the foundation of existential philosophy. The major object of repression, the libido of classical psychoanalysis, was replaced with anxiety and death. Following the philosophy of Martin Heidegger, human being is seen not as a thing, but as a perceptive and responsive openness, the restriction of which results in illness and disturbance. This existential foundation is reflected in a different way of being with a patient. Everything that arises in the relationship is to be seen not as a symbolic account of a drama of underlying forces, something to be interpreted in the light of theory, but as something to be taken seriously as the truth and reality of the patient's existence. The transference relationship is also seen as a genuine interpersonal relationship, not merely a canvas for interpreting past stories.

The towering figure in the main field of humanistic psychology was Abraham Maslow, who was instrumental in turning away from the medical model towards a field of growth and human potential. The origins of his work came from consideration of individuals whom he saw as functioning supremely well, to see if these models could lead him towards any conclusions about the healthy human which would be of help to the less healthy. This led to his theories of the hierarchy of human needs and the process of self-actualisation. He concluded that growth itself is a self-motivating experience and a natural tendency, which will occur whenever it is not blocked by other perceived dangers. He believed Freud's greatest discovery to be the realisation that much psychological illness is caused by the fear of self-knowledge.

The first hierarchy of needs, those factors necessary for natural healthy self-actualisation, are those he called the *deficiency needs*, which are concerned with basic homeostasis, physical necessities and security, and psychological necessities of love and esteem. When these are met, he felt that a further level of needs comes into play, which he termed *being needs*: needs for value and meaning. These, he claimed, are instinctoid in nature and absolutely necessary for the avoidance of illness and the attainment of the full potential of humanness. Indeed, Maslow was later to go further, and finally suggested that spiritual needs are a biological necessity.

This led to the creation of a fourth school, that of Transpersonal Psychology.

Many individual therapies shelter under the huge umbrella of humanistic psychology. Another important name is that of Carl Rogers, who founded the person-centred approach which is central to much of counselling training. Rogers felt that there were three conditions which characterised the person-centred approach, and these have altered the face of therapy and counselling as they relate to the presence of the therapist. The first is congruence or genuineness. It is essential for the therapist to be real and open in the encounter. The second is unconditional positive regard, the manner in which the therapist facilitates a receptive, non-judgemental and accepting attitude towards whatever the client brings to the office. The third is empathic understanding, which means that the therapist should attempt to enter the client's world, sensing as accurately as possible the feelings and meanings that the client is experiencing, and communicating them back to the client in a clarifying reflection. All these add up to listening of a particular skilful kind, and to a stance and a power structure within the therapy which is quite different from that of psychoanalysis, and which has changed the face of much therapy. As we see, the "patient" has now become the "client", which reflects this change in attitude.

Also found within this broad school are therapies which take profound notice of the body and of psychosomatic unity. Exercises using bodily postures, breathing and so forth are used to expose and release energetic blocks. While Freud had actually written of the ego as a mental projection of the surface of the body, he had not followed this up with exploration, and psychoanalysis had become very largely concerned only with verbal and cognitive interactions (Freud, 1923, p. 16). Bringing together the humanistic concern with affect and with the body, Eugene Gendlin created a form of attentional training called Focusing, which sets out to access what he calls the "felt sense". In his own words:

> A felt sense is something you do not at first recognise—it is vague and murky. It feels meaningful, but not known. It is a body sense of meaning. When you learn how to focus, you will discover that the body finding its own way provides its own answers to many of your problems. [1981, p. 10]

He set up a six-step method for accessing and listening to this felt sense, saying that in the movement from the implicit to the explicit the feeling changes, and it is in effecting this movement that the value of psychotherapy lies. Like Maslow, Gendlin came to his theory through studying evidence of thousands of therapy clients and extrapolating what he thought were common factors in those who most benefited from it. He found that the difference between success and failure lay largely in the extent to which clients were able to access bodily those preconscious, subtle, unverbalised feelings and bring them into awareness and verbal expression.

These important changes in the relationship of therapist and client, the emphasis on awareness rather than theory, a belief in essential health and potential, a focus on psychosomatic unity and the importance of existential and interpersonal reality have changed psychotherapies of all persuasions.

The final division is that of Transpersonal Psychology, which was founded by the same Maslow who initiated humanistic psychology. In 1968 he had written: "I consider Humanistic Third Force Psychology to be transitional, a preparation to a still 'higher' Fourth Psychology, transpersonal, transhuman, centred in the cosmos rather than in human needs and interest, going beyond humanness, identity, self-actualisation and the like" (p. iii). This opened the door of psychotherapy to spirituality, Eastern awareness practices, expanded states of consciousness, and assumptions of the potential of human development that go beyond common definitions of normality.[3] It also expanded the Humanistic belief in an innate healthiness, to include spiritual concepts of potential health such as Buddhist ideas of Buddha Nature. Behind the contemporary face of transpersonal psychology were two early godfathers, C. G. Jung and William James. Jung had broken away from Freud because he could not support the centrality of the instinctive libido in unconscious. He became assured that there was an "authentic religious function in the unconscious" and set out his theories of a collective unconscious, beyond the individual receptacle of repression, filled with archetypes, or motifs of collective meaning. Rather than the result of an instinctual struggle, Jung saw psychoneurosis as the "suffering of a soul which has not discovered its meaning" (1958, vol. 11, para. 497).

In the very early days of psychology, before consciousness was relegated to the realms of mysticism and denied a place in a fully scientific psychology, William James had brought together philosophy, psychology and religious meaning in his phenomenological researches. It is interesting to note that more than half a century before transpersonal psychology came into existence as a named school, James had written that "most people live, whether physically, intellectually or morally, in a very restricted circle of their potential being. They make use of a very small portion of their possible consciousness... We all have reservoirs of life to draw upon, of which we do not dream" (1981).

We can note that through the developing history of psychotherapy, there has been an expansion of the territory from intrapsychic to interpersonal and to transpersonal concerns. Each new development has built upon, or in reaction to, its predecessors. Thus in practice today, most therapies are to a greater or lesser extent integrative. Even while the approach may be founded upon one specific outlook, the foundational theories of Freud, of Jung and of object relations, and the practical changes of the humanistic school, the person-centred approach of Rogers, and the technique of focusing have become parts of widely different approaches. The trend towards integration and eclecticism is growing along with an increased emphasis on both multicultural and spiritual perspectives.

How psychotherapy actually works: the neuroscienfitic explanation

All these therapies have over the years considered themselves effective. Such efficacy has been experientially rather than experimentally validated. The few useful studies there have been have mostly had one, perhaps puzzling thing in common: they have found the relationship with the therapist to be of greater importance than their theoretical outlook. Today research from emotional development and attachment theory may be beginning to show us exactly how and why good therapy is helpful. Concern with emotion and the promotion of affect regulation is central to all psychotherapies. We have seen that in early natural development, patterns are physically instantiated in the brain, and that due to neuroplasticity corrections may be made in later life, and change can be achieved alongside the growth of new networks. The individual brain, an organ of adaptation originally shaped by experience during development, may be remodelled during psychotherapy. Psychotherapy may provide an enriched environment which can foster the development of emotional, cognitive and behavioural abilities that were lacking in early childhood. It may act, in short, as a kind of re-parenting.

Research suggests that repair may depend on a kind of re-integration. As the mother or caregiver modelled modes of emotional regulation for the infant, the therapist does likewise, by providing a safe place where emotions may be activated or re-activated, and talked about in order to put them into a new context. Not for nothing was psychoanalysis named the "talking cure". The process of putting feelings into words and the creation of a verbal, narrative self is crucial to emotional security. The infant who lacked encouragement and modelling to put bodily experience into words may not develop the capacity to organise his or her own feelings in adulthood without relying on others. Listening to and telling stories brings together behaviour, affect, sensation and awareness in a manner that enhances the integration of many neural networks. It also enables integration of right and left hemispheres, and such integration corresponds to mental health. Yet talking and interpretation alone is not enough. Talking is but one stage of the process. Any therapist knows that however good their interpretation of the client's process may be, unless the client themselves affectively experiences what they are talking about, no change will occur. Emotions not only affect the way we feel, they also affect the way we remember. Traumatic events charged with emotion will probably be those memories which remain most strongly and for the longest time in an unwanted manner. In therapy we may learn to revisit such charged memories in a different and safe setting, which will not only divorce the memory from the unwanted emotional charge but also rewire the neural associations. Change requires somatic, affective and cognitive experience. The client must have a felt sense of his own body, experience an emotional experience in time with the therapist, and go through the experience of reflecting on these.

Current research would seem to be emphasizing the importance of relationship rather than interpretation in healing. Treatment must match the level of development of the client. The earlier and more severe the pathology, the more the healing emphasis needs to be on relational interventions rather than verbal interpretations (Schore,

2003b, vol. 2). By bringing attention to an emotion in the therapeutic setting, allowing the full experience of it, somatic and affective, in a safe and non-judgemental space, it may be fully acknowledged, a necessary step before integrating it in a new narrative. In this manner, integration of dissociated neural networks is facilitated. Integration is both vertical and horizontal: vertical between subcortical and cortical, the early emotional core of the brain and the later conscious centres, and horizontal between the emotional networks predominantly of the right hemisphere and the semantic processing of the left. So the therapeutic situation may reproduce the ideal childhood scenario in a new, healthful manner. Forming a relationship with an other who listens to how you feel helps you to bring awareness to blocks in feeling and enables you to find words to form a narrative that provides a context for your feelings, and encourages neural integration and the restoration of a healthy flow of experience. Such a setting fosters the integration of conceptual knowledge with emotional and somatic experience in the context of narratives co-constructed with the therapist, just as early experience is ideally co-constructed with the responsive caregiver. What occurs experientially fosters physiological and biochemical change, which in turn aids behavioural and emotional change.

This empathic attunement towards the client is finally becoming explicit. References to it have occurred throughout the history of psychotherapy, and it has been described by many terms such as transference, holding and containment. Freud himself wrote (1912) that the analyst should "turn his own unconscious like a receptive organ towards the transmitting unconscious of the patient. He must adjust himself to the patient as a telephone receiver is adjusted to the transmitting microphone." Freud also recommended that the analyst engage a state of evenly hovering attention, while Bion wrote of "eschewing memory and desire". Schore, relying on neurobiological research as we have noted, describes similarities in interactions between infant and caregiver and between therapist and client in terms of affective transmissions between the right hemispheres in the members of the dyad. He says nonverbal transference and countertransference interactions take place at preconscious levels and represent "right hemisphere to right hemisphere communications of fast-acting, automatic, regulated and unregulated emotional states of patient and therapist" (2002). A fascinating paper from a psychoanalytic perspective talks in terms more familiar, I would have thought, to Buddhist-inspired trainings than traditional psychoanalysis, of "tolerating not-knowing and ambiguity" and of "tuning in" (Stevens, no date). The author describes how the therapist can become an instrument to be "played upon" by the client; saying that this is a technique which can be learned and practised. In two Buddhist-inspired psychotherapy training courses whose philosophical foundations allow them explicitly to explore the idea of intersubjectivity, it is called "exchange", "relational field" and "joint practice".[4] For those who have been exposed to Buddhist practices, there is a two thousand year history of such practices as resource.

Psychotherapy and Buddhism[5]

Psychotherapy of almost all kinds is a process whereby through attention, analysis and language a deeper experience is sought: a personal realisation through which change and transformation may occur. This has been the foundation for the dialogue between Buddhism and psychotherapy. The beginnings of psychotherapy and the introduction of Buddhism into the West occurred around the same time. Following interest in the visit of a Zen Buddhist teacher, Shaku Soen, to the first World Conference of Religions in 1893, D. T. Suzuki came to the United States as secretary to Paul Carus, an early Buddhist writer. Suzuki was introduced to the work of Carus' friend, the psychologist William James, and thus his writings, which were so influential in the introduction of Buddhism—and particularly Zen—to the West, were imbued with a psychological interpretation. This influence has continued. An early translator of one of the books of the Buddhist canon entitled her translation *A Buddhist Manual of Psychological Ethics*, and wrote: "Buddhism from a quite early stage of its development set itself to analyse and classify mental processes with remarkable insight and sagacity. And on the results of that psychological analysis it sought to base the whole rationale of its practical doctrine and discipline" (Rhys Davids 1974, introduction).

In the 1930s Carl Jung wrote psychological commentaries to accompany German translations of two major Tibetan Buddhist works, and also wrote an introduction to a German edition of D. T. Suzuki's *Introduction to Zen Buddhism*. Although Jung was always extremely wary of the dangers of Eastern texts and practices for Westerners, he was impressed by them and aware of their relevance for therapists, writing of Zen that

> The psychotherapist who is seriously concerned with the question of the aim of his therapy cannot remain unmoved when he sees the end towards which this Eastern method of psychic healing—i.e. "making whole"—is striving. As we know, this question has occupied the most adventurous minds of the East for more than two thousand years, and in this respect methods and philosophical doctrines have been developed which simply put all Western attempts along those lines into the shade. [1958, vol. 11, para. 905]

Since that time the dialogue has continued uninterrupted. In 1950s D. T. Suzuki was still a central figure in the debate, and with Erich Fromm and Richard de Martino was one of the co-authors of an influential book, *Zen Buddhism and Psychoanalysis*, which came out of a conference of the same name in Mexico City in 1957. In the 1960s the field broadened considerably with the Tibetan diaspora and the beginning of the popularisation of Buddhist ideas by such writers as Alan Watts. Today the stream of books linking Buddhism and psychotherapy has become a flood. In 1960 Alan Watts claimed to have read everything written in this field. Today this would hardly be possible. From scholarly comparisons with Western scientific research to so-called Buddhist tips on dating the shelves are filled. Many Buddhist meditators have become psychotherapists and have continued to develop the dialogue.[6] From the other direction, some traditional teachers have given their teaching a psychological slant and directed them specifically towards an audience of therapists and healers.[7]

The reasons for this lie in the very nature of the concerns of both disciplines. Some are timeless while others, which I am particularly interested in here, come specifically from an ever-increasing congruence between changing paradigms and problems within Western thought and lives, and Buddhist Dharma. Of the former—let us say fundamental—reasons, the most evident is a shared focus upon experience. This is at the heart of Buddhism, where the principal aim is the true understanding of the human condition, and in the wake of such understanding, the adoption of a different way of life leading to liberation from suffering. Buddhist teachings, as we will see in more detail, present an experiential psychology which both reveals and rests upon a philosophy of process. This philosophy is empirical and its aim is liberative and psychotherapeutic: to transform ourselves cognitively and emotionally in accordance with the Buddha's awakened understanding of the way experience occurs. Thus liberation from suffering is to be achieved through understanding the nature of suffering. Unlike other religions or philosophies, Buddhism is far less concerned with ontology, with *what* exists, than with an exploration of *how* things exist.

The method of considering experience is through analysis of mind and mind states. A major text of early Buddhism, the *Dhammapada* (translated by Byrom, 1976), begins:

> We are what we think:
> All that we are arises with our thoughts.
> With our thoughts we make the world.
> Speak or act with an impure mind
> And trouble will follow you
> As the wheel follows the ox that draws the cart.

> We are what we think:
> All that we are arises with our thoughts.
> With our thoughts we make the world.
> Speak or act with a pure mind
> And happiness will follow you
> As your shadow, unshakeable.

Following on from this recognition of the importance of mind, Buddhism provides over two thousand years' experience of the methodical and phenomenological study of mind. Arising from this, it presents practices for the cultivation of desirable mental habits and emancipation from undesirable ones. Such practices arise hand in hand with the philosophical theories which underwrite them, each mutually dependent upon the other, in a far more integral manner than is found in the West, where theory and practice have become ever more separated. In the East, personal cultivation has always been a fundamental part of traditional philosophy.

At this time however, I believe that the specific relevance of Buddhist exploration of mind to the West is stronger than ever: for therapists working practically with suffering human beings, for neuroscientists seeking to find a basis for scrupulous exploration of subjective consciousness, and for ordinary people trying to find happiness in a world of ever-increasing change and uncertainty. The West has been undergoing enormous changes both in belief and in lifestyle. Discoveries such as relativity, indeterminacy and quantum mechanics in the scientific field; cubism and abstraction and conceptualism in art; and stream of consciousness writing and deconstruction theory have brought about a metaphysical shift which clashes with earlier frames of reference. There has been a swing away from naïve realism towards understanding both world and knowledge as a dynamic and interdependent process: our knowledge is no longer considered as sheer representation, a mirror image of an externally existing reality, but is becoming acknowledged as a construction, an implicative enaction arising from cognitive and embodied interaction with world. Concern with mechanism has shifted to concern with organism, from linear causality to circular causality, from representation to implication and engagement with complexity and chaos.

We live in a climate of belief which affects not only scientists but also all of us. The media constantly refer to the postmodern, but what does this mean? On the one hand it is merely what follows the modern. But whereas the modern was a time of experimentation and of hope, the postmodern is both older and more adolescent, more knowing, more ironic and more cynical. It is too wise to trustingly accept everything at face value, but is equally the victim of its own scepticism, in danger of not being able to accept anything at all. Suffering the loss of all certainty, it is at risk of losing all hope. If there is one prevailing existential feature of the postmodern, it is fragmentation. In literature we find fragmentation of identity, of perspective and of story; in architecture, buildings in a medley of styles, ironically commentating one on another; in philosophy, the deconstruction of previous foundations for certainty. If we compare our daily lives today with those of earlier times, there is this same detachment. The majority of people in the wealthy "north" live divorced from natural cycles. Electricity has freed us from the time of dawn and dusk. We are increasingly urbanised or suburbanised; seasons pass without profound acknowledgement of their change: heating goes on in the winter and air conditioning in the summer at the flick of a switch. Lives and work continue largely untouched by the background of weather.

Perhaps the greatest fragmentation of the postmodern has been the fragmentation of meaning itself. The most often quoted definition of the postmodern is Lyotard's "incredulity towards metanarratives" (1986, p. xxiv). Though this is not the subject of casual conversation outside the academy, it reflects a general feeling that is. The overarching certainties of religion and philosophy have come under attack and crumbled as never before. Even as we see the impossibility of certainty and singular identity, we still grasp them. In the words of a contemporary writer: "It seems to me that certainty, and the need for identity which it serves, is a sort of virulent and dangerous disease. Yet it becomes equally clear that the need for it is the deepest impulse there is" (Lott, 1996, p. 205).

There are two main responses to such need and such uncertainty: to close down our experience of uncertainty and cling to fundamentalist belief closed to rational analysis and criticism, or to grasp the nettle and open up to a new response to new contexts. Such shifts require the courage to engage with a different philosophy and different narratives. As Western ideas move away theoretically from traditional metaphysical dualisms (appearance-reality, mind-body, objective-subjective) and experience the breakup of many of the grand metanarratives which have until recently supported Western belief systems, they show greater compatibility with Buddhist process philosophy. Buddhist philosophy, always essentially different from that of the modern West, may resonate more fully in some ways with the postmodern. At the foundation of this philosophy is a view of the interdependent origination of all phenomena. According to Buddhist thought, this network of interdependent origination rests in emptiness, the transparency or lack of essential unchanging essence in all phenomena, including persons. Such a philosophy resonates with the postmodern world we now inhabit in the West: resonates both with the science of chaos and dynamic systems theory and with the social world and the fragmented selves of our experience.

It is the emphasis in Buddhism on practice which is especially important for psychotherapy and for working with the emotions. Most importantly, the Buddhist view does not separate theory from practice and daily experience. The models of causality and of human being are undertaken in order to show how things occur, not what they consist of. Through understanding how the world is, how its processes work and how we perceive or misperceive them, we may live better and more happily. The outlook and practices provide a path. This path is a middle way, a centred understanding free of the major dualities which have for so long structured Western thought. Subjective-objective, inner-outer, self-world, mind-body and life-death become interrelated and interdependent rather than exclusive in a logic of complementarity rather than of contradiction. Over the years, Western civilisation has relied upon these fundamental dualisms which have indelibly marked our culture to an extent that we are now often quite unaware of them.[8] The very fact of such basic dualities as, for example, self-other, mind-body, cognition-emotion and life-death are, I suggest, less important than the value judgements we have added to them. Self has become far more important than other, mind valued far above body, cognition valued beyond emotion. And so we have lost balance and lost connection.

Buddhist practices, based on its first psychology, may provide a great resource for the contemporary psychotherapy we need. For, as explained earlier, Buddhism can offer us a very long history of the subjective exploration of experience, a subtle and experiential psychology of mind, and an understanding of the interdependence of mind and world. Buddhism sees human being not as having a fixed and unchanging essence but as comprising a set of processes which may be developed and transformed. It presents a philosophy in service to a practice which leads to a better way of being in the world. In furtherance of this end, philosophy, psychology and ethics all come together in a multi-layered and multidisciplinary enterprise. Above all, it has more than two thousand years' history of experiential awareness practices.

Notes

1. The title of a book on later developments in psychoanalysis, *Mothering Psychoanalysis*, encapsulates a lack in the Freudian approach, and describes later attempts to redress this. Many years after Freud, French feminist psychoanalysts such as Julia Kristeva, Helene Cixous and Luce Irigaray also addressed this aspect of psychoanalysis.

2. For the sake of simplicity I will write of mother and infant, being aware that this may relate to either parent, or indeed to the primary caregivers.

3. See J. Welwood, *The Meeting of the Ways* and *The Awakening of the Heart;* R. Walsh & F. Vaughan, *Beyond Ego;* D. Goleman, *The Meditative Mind;* G. Claxton, *Beyond Therapy.*

4. These are the Contemplative Psychotherapy program at Naropa University, Boulder, CO, and the Core Process Psychotherapy Training offered by the Karuna Institute in Devon, UK.

5. I have written at length about the relationship between Buddhism and psychotherapy in an earlier work (1998).

6. For example: Mark Epstein, Joseph Goldstein, John Welwood, James Low, Karen Kissel Wegela.

7. For example: Tarthang Tulku at the Nyingma Institute in Berkeley, CA; Trungpa Rinpoche, who set up the Naropa Institute (now a university) in Boulder, CO.

8. Interestingly, the bivalent orientation of Western thinking has quite recently been challenged by what is called Fuzzy Logic, a multivalued or "vague" logic based on a continuum of degree rather than exclusivity. A recent book on the subject points out that a map of those areas in which research on fuzzy logic is respected and widespread is closely comparable to a map of the areas in which Buddhist thought flourished. Such thinking was largely rejected in the West until the results of its beneficial application in technological contexts (such as washing machines and dryers) became impossible to ignore. See Kosko (1994).

CHAPTER FOUR

The earliest explanation: the Buddhist view

Pilgrimage ... becomes a journey from ordinary perception into full consciousness of our interpretive role in determining reality, to recognize, as Padmasambhava states, that all phenomena are in essence the magical display of mind.

(Baker, 2004)

Unlike other religions, Buddhism acknowledges neither a creator God nor a set of beliefs that demand allegiance. It offers instead a close exploration of our mind, an experiential psychology, which demonstrates that things are not exactly how we immediately and innately believe them to be. Corresponding to the results of this questioning process, it offers practices intended to bring about cognitive and emotional transformation. Such practices lead us to conform to the way things really are rather than the way we innately believe them to be. Thus Buddhism presents us with a philosophy of process and a psychological guide to living well in accordance with such a philosophy. It is a guide to help us both on the spiritual journey and also on that of our everyday lives, health and happiness.

First we must realise that there are many "Buddhisms". Tibetan Buddhism is very different from the Theravada approach of Sri Lanka, which differs in detail from the same system of Burma or Thailand. Japanese Buddhism itself embraces many forms; Zen is very different from Pure Land. The major distinctions are those of Early Buddhism, the teachings of the Sutras, whose closest contemporary practitioners are those of the Theravada approach, Mahayana, or the Great Way of later Buddhism, and Vajrayana, the Diamond Way of Tibetan Buddhism. Yet at the centre they share a core which is sufficiently unchanging for them all to shelter under one umbrella term "Buddhism". What they share at heart is a concern with a way of living as disclosed by the historical Buddha, with a practical concern with action as more important than theory. In a recent interview the Dalai Lama, answering the question "What is the essence of Buddhism?" replied: "Respect for all forms of life, and then compassion and affection towards all sentient beings, with the understanding that everything is interdependent—so my happiness and suffering, my wellbeing, very much have to do with other Is."[1] He denied that Buddhism was centrally concerned with chanting and rituals or with philosophy, stating: "The dharma, it's just the mind." He continued to explain that he felt that belief in recitation and rituals may in fact cause us to neglect the basic instruments that actually transform the mind, stating that such instruments are the altruistic spirit of enlightenment (bodhicitta),[2] the transcendent attitude, renunciation, the realisation of impermanence, and the wisdom of selflessness.

The very bone structure of Early Buddhism is the teaching of the Four Noble Truths, or better said, the four ennobling truths that present a skeletal structure from which all associated teachings proceed. They are very commonly presented as statements, as facts. Closer examination of the sutra or teaching in which they were first presented, the Buddha's first public talk after his enlightenment, called the Sutra of the Turning of the Wheel of Dharma, discloses that they were presented in the form of actions to be followed. The intention of Buddhism, the teaching of the Awakened One, is to provide a path, a way to understand phenomena properly and to live in accordance with this knowledge, so that we may escape the otherwise inevitable suffering.

The first truth, as we have seen, is that of awareness that all of life as habitually lived, in Sanskrit samsara, is unsatisfactory. It entails anguish and stress. This fact is "to be known". Our first duty is to acknowledge this, to acknowledge that the very nature of life is unsatisfactory as we ordinarily place ourselves in relation to it. This suffering or unsatisfactoriness is described as ordinary suffering. There is also the suffering of illness, and ultimately the suffering of death. The existential fact of our inevitable death, so often evaded, is the mark of ultimate unsatisfactoriness from the point of view of our own bounded, individual life. Interestingly, this point is emphasised by science. "Any project for human salvation—any project capable of turning a life examined into a life contented—must include ways to resist the anguish conjured up by suffering and death, cancel it, and substitute joy instead" (Damasio, 2003, p. 271).

The other truths are there to lead us away from anguish. How? Not by ignoring it or by distraction, our usual patterns, but by acknowledging it. It is to be seen clearly, its causes are to be learnt, and we are encouraged to understand that we do have some choices. We can transform our instinctual reactions into wise responses. We can learn to cultivate healthy emotions, weaken afflictive ones. We are given a path to lead us to liberation from suffering and to wellbeing.

The second truth refers to the cause of this unsatisfactoriness. The action asked of us is to cease creating this cause. Suffering or unsatisfactoriness arises from what is usually given as the emotional cause of desire. In its positive form this is easy to see. We want something; we know that to possess these new clothes, this house, this new love or job or haircut will change our lives for the better. Negatively it is less clear. We do not desire, we actively push away those things, those experiences that threaten us, or are not part of the image with which we wish to identify. However, the actual word the Buddha used in his first talk was not the common word for desire but one more usually translated as thirst or craving, which represents more than just desire. It includes our reaction to, and identification with, desire or aversion.[3] I think we can easily notice how all this craving and pushing away is in the service of the self, or more precisely, the self image. We desire to bolster this thing, the self with which we identify. We see it as permanent and solid, and do not realise that from the Buddhist perspective it is constructed and changeable and empty. In our contemporary society we are ever more alienated from appreciating its actual interrelationship and dependence on a network of causes and conditions.

This demand to cease craving is a very hard one for a culture of consumption to hear. Daily we are bombarded by the commercial message that desire is good and consumption better; that we exist to shop and define ourselves by our purchases. Buddhism acknowledges this but sees it not as a beneficial goal, an escape from what is unsatisfactory, but as a fundamental error, a false medicine, the cause of a cycle of unending suffering rather than its cure.

This is the very stuff of psychotherapy. It is the very material of narcissism, of the concern with self-image, the ever-increasing tide of desire in the service of bolstering the self-image, the endless struggle to fill the inner emptiness that results from the loss of connection. Even when we find happiness, how strongly we cling to it, how little we want to let it go. Buddhism speaks of the suffering of pain, suffering of change and impermanence and the suffering of conditions, the inevitable suffering that arises from the contingency of our lives and our implication in a world compounded of unreliable and unstable conditions.

If the emotional cause which leads to the second truth of the arising of suffering is desire, the cognitive cause is ignorance or misperception. This is ignorance or confusion about the way things, both phenomena and selves, really come to be. Buddhism delineates ignorance most precisely as being ignorance or confusion regarding three fundamental marks or attributes of existence. The first is that everything, to greater or lesser extent, is impermanent. We cannot stop the process, the endless ongoing flow of life and experience which will inevitably lead on the personal level to our own death and on a great scale to the birth and death of cosmos. Secondly, because of this, life entails unsatisfactoriness. No sooner do we have what we want than the moment passes, the toy breaks, we become ill, eventually we die. Thirdly, everything is essentially without self. What does this mean? It refers to the central Buddhist teachings concerning interdependence and emptiness. The two are inextricably linked. The first is called the teaching of dependent origination or dependent co-arising (*pratitya samutpada*). The Buddha saw in his moment of enlightenment the truth that all phenomena are interconnected. All phenomena are dependent upon a network of causes and conditions. Nothing is utterly isolated or independent. As I sit here writing, I am physically supported by my parentage, a whole network of my genetic heritage, the air I breathe, the food I ate for breakfast. This in turn involves all those who harvested the wheat and made the bread, the sun and the rain that nurtured the wheat, and so on.[4] Less tangibly, culturally the form I take is dependent upon the society within which I was raised, the books I have read, the teachings I have heard, and so forth. Rather than a solid self, I am the presentation of an ever-changing display of physical and mental processes dependent on an ever-spreading network of connections, normally totally unacknowledged, in the centre (for me) of which I sit. And there's the rub. Each of us tends to think of ourselves as the independent, isolated, solid centres of individual experiential universes. In this central hub of the web we sit like spiders, considering all that comes into our web as a resource for us. Each web is our own egocentric universe. This view leads to the suffering of which the first truth speaks: the unsatisfactoriness, the stress that we should truly acknowledge.

A particular version of this general theory of dependent origination shows a twelve-step cycle by which life in thrall to ignorance arises. It delineates a progression from consciousness to belief in isolated independence, on through ever increasingly emotional grasping to endless cycles of birth and death within illusion, which is life as we commonly know it and live it (samsara). Ignorance of the true relational existence of self is the cognitive cause of suffering. Arising from such misconception, we seek through the mechanisms of desire and aversion to fortify or defend that misconceived isolated sense of self which never truly existed in the first place.

The later Mahayana Buddhist presentation of emptiness arises from this philosophy of interdependence. It states that all phenomena are empty of essential, isolated and permanent "selves" or essence — because they are constructed, composite and interdependent. All phenomena, including, as we have seen, our selves, are dependent upon a web of causes and conditions. Thus "emptiness" is not the emptiness of privation, the narcissistic emptiness of lack we meet in the therapy office, but is in fact a recontextualization, a belonging, an openness of dependence upon a vast richness. One of the most beautiful symbols in Buddhism, one that is increasingly being cited in contemporary Western texts, is that of the net of the god Indra. It describes an endless net that has a jewel at every intersection. Every jewel reflects every other jewel in every facet, and is itself reflected in every facet of every other jewel, presenting an endless co-emergent, co-dependent glory. Indra's net is a safety net of interdependence that holds us, allowing us to balance midway between nothingness and essentialism.

With regard to our selves, the fact that we are not a solid unchanging self, but rather a set of processes, offers hope. For, rather than existing as solidity and unchanging permanence, we present a set of skills which may be improved and transformed. A rare Western appreciation of this (and a surprisingly Buddhist-sounding one) comes from a recent work by the neuropsychologist Paul Broks: "Minds emerge from process and interaction, not substance. In a sense, we inhabit the spaces between things. We subsist in emptiness. A beautiful, liberating thought and nothing to be afraid of" (2003, p. 57). This hope is reflected in the third truth. It is the truth which states that there is a way out. There may be liberation from entrapment in suffering, unsatisfactoriness and stress. This truth of liberation is not merely to be known cognitively, but is to be realized, realized in body, speech and mind, physically, emotionally and cognitively, through all the doors of our experience.

The fourth truth refers to the path, a path of eight steps which is "to be cultivated". For, as I said earlier, Buddhism does not provide so much a set of beliefs but a *way*, a way of cultivation and practice in the service of transformation. Again, this is a complete transformation that involves body, speech and mind, embodiment, emotion, imagination and cognition in the service of eudaimonia, flourishing of self and others. The eight steps of the path—right intention, right thought, speech, action, livelihood, mindfulness, concentration and wisdom—are conventionally divided into three main groupings: those of wisdom, morality and meditation. The path of wisdom relates to the wisdom that understands the fundamental truths of interdependence and emptiness. Inseparable from such wisdom, compassion arises. From a truly embodied understanding of these truths, morality arises. For this is an ethic of compassion and interconnectedness, an ethic of responsibility and response-ability. It is a shift away from an ego-centred approach to the world, a confrontation with the world from the isolated axis of my own individual and unconnected centre, to a stance of engagement and of realisation of mutual dependence, concern and interconnection.

The third division of the path, meditation, refers to intention, mindfulness and concentration. These, along with compassion, are the practices to be cultivated. These are the ways we may experientially question our own understanding and deconstruct our moment-to-moment arising experience. By learning how to come to the "witness" position, rather than being entirely absorbed and swept away by our experience, we may come to understand how we frame it and how we close down this moment-to-moment awareness, this rising and falling, this impermanence, this "emptiness" to oppose the flow of process, a solid structure of things and self. Understanding this, and practising different ways of being, we may transform ourselves. Sitting meditation curtails physical doing and limits mental doing. The normal action-observation-action loop is interrupted, which changes the focus of awareness from awareness of specific features to a wider non-feature awareness. In the absence of an action programme, all the mind has as its focus is the state of the system itself. Such a change of focus, a revision of mind and self, creates the opportunity for new structure to form.[5] More specifically, having attained such changes by concentrative meditation, other branches of Buddhism, such as Tibetan Vajrayana, offer practices of carefully chosen visualizations designed to induce changes in associations and emotional response.[6]

To follow this path does not mean we have to totally give up our ordinary way of being in the world. It does mean we should no longer see it as the only way. It allows us to lessen our tight grip on the world and on ourselves. It encourages us to open up to wider understanding: that with more faith in the whole needing less reliance on self, we can become *more* responsible for what is other, more compassionate to others and more compassionate to self. It shows us the inseparability of conventional and absolute truths, the way the world exists conventionally to us, and the understanding that ultimately such understanding is misplaced. As a scientist may see a table, knowing simultaneously that while at the quantum level the table is made up of moving particles, she can functionally lean on it to write her theoretical description of its micro-structure, so Buddhism can help us live more compassionately, more happily in the ordinary world, while encouraging us to desolidify our view of both world and self. The emptiness of which Buddhism speaks is far from the emptiness to which our consumerism and our materialistic philosophy have led us. Buddhism's deconstruction of phenomena and self does not lead to the emptiness of lack, but liberates us from the suffering, stress and unsatisfactoriness of trying to create and protect something which does not exist, never existed, and never will exist: an isolated, independent life. To give up the struggle is not to give up life and self; it is to find it, enriched in its interconnection.

Buddhist philosophy and practice is fundamentally experiential. It embodies an attempt to set down a way of life which is in accord with the ways things really come to be. The discovery of this reality rests on profound exploration of the way we construct our experience. Thus Buddhism may be said to present the earliest "psychology". It is not concerned with ontology, with what exists, but rather with how anything exists, with epistemology and psychology, with the manner in which our minds (and our bodies) construct our experience. The stream of consciousness as it arises in the present moment and is known to an attentive and carefully trained observer provides the field of investigation.[7] Buddhist psychology presents various models of mind, of knowing and of selves who know. All of these are process models, describing the construction of known reality and of selves moment by moment. Their most important features are those of impermanence, process and construction.

One central model tracks the construction of all experience through one of the six sense systems. In Buddhist models mind, or mental perception, appears as a sixth sense organ. All experience occurs through a three-way interaction between a sense organ which is called a sense door (sight, sound, smell, taste, touch or cognition), a sensory object (data from the environment to which the organ is receptive), and a moment of knowing the object, of perception by means of a corresponding consciousness. All of our experience according to Buddhist psychology is constructed from these eighteen elements: six sense doors, six sense objects and six modes of consciousness.

Another process model describes the construction of the knower, the sentient being who knows, who is created out of the coming together of five aggregates. This is an interdependent process of the material or physical dimension called *form*; an affective component, *feelings*, which represents those primary feelings which move our attention towards objects with desire, aversion or indifference; a cognitive component usually translated as *perception*;

a somewhat complex aggregate called *dispositions* or *formations*, which comprises patterns of intention and predispositions; and *consciousness*. I will consider this model more fully in the chapter on selves.

All these models set out to illustrate the constructed and procesual nature of the self. Selves are neither permanent nor independent. Understanding this emptiness of isolation and fixture, this space of potential, this interdependence, gives rise to compassion. Tibetan Buddhism emphasises the twin pillars of wisdom and compassion. Wisdom is this understanding of interdependence from which arises compassion, which embraces a rather more dynamic concept than our usual Western use of the word. It is sometimes translated as "skilful means" and designates the caring action that arises from true understanding of our non-separation.

Two further important models from Mahayana, or later Buddhism are those of the three kayas, bodies or realms, and of Buddha Nature, or innate health.[8] The *Dharmakaya*, realm or body of truth, is that of pristine awareness and emptiness from which all arises; the *Sambhogakaya*, body of enjoyment, denotes the level of energy through which emptiness reveals itself; the *Nirmanakaya*, or level of emanation, is the material manifestation of phenomena. The three kayas are actually an indivisible unity: just as form and emptiness cannot be separated, nor can the kayas. As with all Buddhist models, these are methods of explaining in one-dimensional form that which is three-dimensional and interconnected. The *Dharmakaya* is the all-pervading mind, the empty awareness that is full of everything. The *Sambhogakaya* relates to the dimension of energy and of communication, which mediates between the resource of the *Dharmakaya* and the actuality of the realm of phenomena. It is the realm of sound and of light, of imagination and archetypes. *Nirmanakaya* is the actual material world of manifestation, the embodiment of energy. This tripartite pattern is seen as functioning in different areas: as described above in the dimension of the awakened state, and under the influence of ignorance in the "normal" threefold model of body, speech and mind. Body corresponds to *Nirmanakaya*; speech, which includes energy, communication, breath and emotion, corresponds to *Sambhogakaya*; and mind—not just intellect, but the mind that has its centre in the heart—corresponds to *Dharmakaya*; a correlation that might also be extended to my three headings of Embodiment, Emotion and

Environment. The threefold division may also be applied both to states of existence and to teachings: as coarse, subtle and very subtle and outer, inner and secret respectively.

Buddha Nature stands for the pure potential health available to us all, the transpersonal unsullied Mind. It is reflected in different psychotherapies as Brilliant Sanity, and Wise Mind.[9] This belief in the potential of health behind every interruption and disturbance of it is a singular characteristic of Buddhist-inspired psychotherapy. It provides a ground for humanistic psychology's belief that, if unchecked, the natural tendency is towards health. Thus it provides a more positive twist to the psychotherapy it inspires, which is strengthened by early Buddhist psychological ideas of supporting wholesome emotions while vitiating the strength of destructive ones. Western psychotherapy, with its early reliance on the medical model, has had a tendency to emphasise suffering and the negative. Only as late as 1999 was the term Positive Psychology coined by a leading US psychologist, Martin Seligman, highlighting a shift towards greater emphasis on building up the positive aspects of our experience.[10] This outlook has been much quoted in the recent emphasis upon happiness in the media.

The major practices presented by Buddhist teachings, as seen in the four ennobling truths, are those of meditation and mindfulness. Meditation has a dual function: it provides the path of revealing for each of us the reality of our constructed experience, and it also allows us to transform ourselves in accordance with this discovery, through cultivation of healthy mind states. If we can see how suffering arises from our grasping and clinging to desires which solidify our sense of self, in ignorance of the impermanence and transparency of that self, with clear sight we can let go of our clinging, and thus of our suffering.

There are two major forms of meditation: concentration and insight. Concentration teaches us how to settle our minds. Insight may then allow us to watch the moment-to-moment arising of our experience, allowing us to see our experience in the light of understanding of impermanence and non-self. Control of our attention is of major importance both for our understanding of reality and for our transformation of ourselves in line with it. William James wrote in 1890 (1981) that

The faculty of voluntarily bringing back a wandering attention over and over again is the very root of judgement, character and will. No one is *compos sui* if he have it not. An education which should improve this faculty would be the education par excellence. [p. 401]

Understanding this and engaging in practices of attention, we may transform ourselves. As we have noted, meditation practice curtails physical "doing" and limits mental "doing". It shifts focus from contents of mind to the way minds work. Even more specifically, the practices of Vajrayana are those of symbolic recreation of one's self, in which carefully chosen imaginative visualizations are designed to induce changes in associations and emotional response. Research is showing that such changes may be long-term, physically instantiated and beneficial to our happiness. Such abilities are seen to be of central importance for psychotherapy in terms of the neuroplasticity, the potential for change, which such research has uncovered.

Notes

1. From an interview with Robert Thurman (5.4.01) reproduced in Tibet Foundation Newsletter no. 32, May 2001.
2. Buddhist terminology is given in Sanskrit, unless stated otherwise.
3. In his recent book *Open to Desire*, Mark Epstein writes most interestingly about this topic.
4. This is beautifully described by Thich Nhat Hanh in *The Heart of Understanding*, p. 3.
5. For an interesting explanation of this see, D. Galin, "The concepts 'self', 'person' and 'I' in Buddhism and in Western psychology", in Wallace (2003).
6. See F. J. Varela & N. Depraz, "Imagining", in Wallace (2003).
7. For a very good short exposition of Buddhist psychology see Andrew Olendzki, "Buddhist Psychology", in Segall (2003).
8. For an excellent and much more detailed explanation see Fremantle (2000), p. 173.
9. Again, the first relates to Contemplative Psychotherapy, the second to Core Process Psychotherapy.
10. Martin Seligman is Director of the University of Pennsylvania Positive Psychology Center. For more information, see www.authentichappiness. sas.upenn.edu.

PART II
MEDITATION

Introduction

The great yogi Milarepa said, "Meditating is not meditating on something, but familiarizing (yourself with your mind)."

(Wangchuk Dorje, Mahamudra, *The Ocean of Definitive Meaning*, p. xivi)

With no object, no image and no focus, what are you looking at? You are looking at you looking.

(Turrell, 1993)[1]

* * *

If our aim is to flourish, to find genuine wellbeing, we need to think of things with a kind of double vision. We should honour the scientific truths about our brains and bodies and accept the way "things really are", letting go of the comforting illusions we cherish: that we are totally in control, fully conscious, in possession of eternal non-physical souls, and so forth. Then this hard knowledge needs to be accompanied by the subjective aspect, the feel of things and the knowledge of what control we do have in practice. Theory and practice, knowledge and experience must come together; the first and third person perspectives need to be aligned.

The term meditation, in Sanskrit *bhavana*, means cultivation, bringing into being. The same term in Tibetan, *sgom*, means familiarisation. Maybe this reflects the way Buddhist thought uses the practice both to reveal our reality and to transform it. In the Buddhist traditions there are two main kinds of meditation practice: concentration leading to focus, and insight or discursive, reflective meditation. It seems that our contemporary Western daily life takes us further and further from this kind of thinking and reflection. We saw earlier that William James considered that control of our attention was vital, and encouraged an education that would develop this faculty (1890/1981, p. 401). Today, over a century later, such an education is even more lacking. We seek entertainment not reflection, we flee from silence and contemplation. Radio, television and music surround our every move. Even the automatic cash machines in the USA blare at us, and runners out in the wild are rarely seen without Walkmen or iPods pumping sound into their ears. The average attention span of a child becomes shorter and shorter, and to accommodate this, the media parcel up their stories in ever smaller soundbites with ever greater emotional ramping up to capture our attention. Space is rarely left for contemplation of what is, or free imagination of what might be. Our minds are so stuffed with content that their own workings are entirely hidden.

The aims of contemplation are just the opposite. Far from filling our minds with action and content, meditation aims to make us stop and familiarise ourselves with the very way our minds work, to encourage self-awareness and self-knowledge for the purpose of self-control and self-creation. Meditation does not refer, as often thought, to some mystical experience. In the words of a contemporary Tibetan teacher, "Meditation in terms of practice is connected to attentiveness. Paying attention is meditation."[2] If we cannot change many of the problems and anguish of external life, we can pay attention, and in so doing we can change our response to them. As the Buddhist saint and scholar Santideva wrote back in the eighth century:

Where would I find enough leather
With which to cover the surface of the earth?
But (wearing) leather just on the soles of my shoes
Is equivalent to covering the earth with it.

Likewise it is not possible for me
To restrain the external course of things;
But should I restrain this mind of mine
What would be the need to restrain all else? [vv. 13–14]

The scientist Paul Ekman, in an afterword to his comprehensive study of emotions (2003), recommends mindful meditation in order to increase awareness of emotional behaviour and impulse. Although he says that at the time of his writing there is no hard scientific evidence that mindfulness meditation (like psychotherapy) improves emotional life, experientially many claim that it does. He also states that the very practice of focusing attention onto an automatic process such as breathing creates the ability to become aware of other automatic processes. Learning to pay attention to formerly non-conscious breathing, as any meditator knows, takes practice. During such practice we will develop new neural pathways, and such skills and pathways become transferable to other automatic processes, such as those of impulse and emotion. As David Siegel succinctly describes, "In mindfulness, we direct our attention to our intention. Where attention goes, neurons fire. And where neurons fire, they can rewire" (2007, p. 291). Thus meditative practice may physically transform our brains and our experience. Indeed, recent research has shown enormous (in some cases over one hundred per cent) difference in neurological activity in the part of the brain concerned with feelings of happiness in the brains of long-term meditators.

So I would like here to follow this path away from our usual distractions, and contemplate, familiarise ourselves with the great changes in science in a reflective manner, trying to pay attention both to the theories and to what they mean to our experience. The topics of our reflective attention will be those most affected by the changes in thought coming from the new science: embodiment, emotion and environment, and the selves which emerge from our interaction with these. Strangely, these divisions reflect quite neatly the ancient Buddhist categories of body, speech and mind from which our selves or non-selves are constructed. Throughout concern with embodiment, emotion and environment, a fourth interwoven theme will emerge: ethics. A weakening, almost to the point of loss, of traditional foundations of morality has been accompanied by a virtually frantic search for a suitable moral code. Maybe, from the new knowledge concerning our deepest natures, we can re-found an ethical stance.

Notes

1. Artist James Turrell, quoted in *Air Mass* exhibition catalogue, Hayward Gallery, London 1993, and repeated in James Turrell Deer Shelter, Yorkshire Sculpture Park, Albion and The Art Fund, 2006.
2. Traleg Kyabgon Rinpoche, "Meditation and Self Transformation", in *Vidyadhara*, Spring 1996, no. 12.

CHAPTER FIVE

Embodiment

The brain's body-furnished, body-minded mind is a servant of the whole body.

(Damasio, 2003, p. 206)

I don't say, "I think, therefore, I am." Rather, I say, "I am embodied; therefore I experience that I am."

(Keleman, 1999, p. 4)

No one is really looking for the meaning of life. People are looking for an experience of life. The home that you came from was an experience of life.

(J. Campbell in Keleman, 1999, p. 75)

Breathe in.
Spring air is sharp at first, sharp and clear at the back of nose and palate, washed with recent rain.
I am sitting on a cushion by the open door of a hut in a garden next to a large pond. As I breathe in I smell the faint hay odour of the tatami mat beneath me. As the sun comes out from behind clouds I feel its warmth on my feet and knees. My eyes crease up against the brightness.

Breathe out.
I feel the air expelled, relief as diaphragm falls. Pause—expectation.
Breathe in.

Pay attention to the body. Sun on my right foot, left in shade,
warmth of wool socks,
sun warming up to the knee where shade begins.
Cushion is cold under my bottom,
thighs and lower back stiff,
shoulders tight and high.
Breathe out and let them fall.
Sun burning on my hand,
dried skin around the nails, irritates, I find I'm fiddling with it
unconsciously.
Consciously I stop.
Breeze on my face,
eyes staring out, watching, wanting to capture the life of the pond
in front.
Ears taking in myriad sounds, birds singing, spring nesting.
Fiddling again with fingers.
Thinking—hands, hand cream, shopping, plans—
floating off on a chain of thought,

body forgotten again.

Come back to body.
Breathe.

Diaphragm expanding,
sense of increase,
the air is fresh,
spring and growth,
and suddenly I am miles away,
in springs of my childhood,
lost in memory and emotion,
in hopes unfulfilled, in shame at lack of achievement,
the present lost,
out of my body,
wallowing with regret
in a world of my own emotions,
cut off from all around and from my present experience.

How often does this happen? From sharp present awareness the world narrows to one constructed and confined by our own worries and thoughts, which constrain any other possibilities with the iron gates of their expectations, their fear, their closure. Our minds have taken over the interpretation of our experience to such an extent that the experiences themselves through the other sense gates, through sight and sound, taste, touch and smell, are forgotten and lost. Meditative reflection encourages us to reconnect with this experience.

Psychotherapy is often seen as a search for meaning. Jung believed all the psychological problems of the second half of life were symptoms of a search for meaning. We had the experience but missed the meaning, as T. S. Eliot wrote. Yet, as Joseph Campbell later pointed out, we are also in danger sometimes of paying so much attention to meaning that we actually miss the experience. In his words we "let the concept swallow up the percept, defending ourselves from the *experience*" (1969, p. 186). For Campbell the duty of the work of art is to evoke in us a *sense of existence* rather than an *assurance of meaning*. Yet it is not an either-or situation; we need both meaning and experience, experience and meaning. Problems arise when we privilege one at the expense of the other. Since Descartes, embodiment has increasingly become the underprivileged term in comparison with mind, our guarantee of existence. Over the years the unchallenged acceptance of "I think, therefore I am" has reduced our bodies to mere vehicles, noticeable only when something has gone wrong. Alternatively, today these reified bodies have become identified with our self-image and have become possessions to be polished, adorned, cherished. Neither seems fully lived in and from. How often do we carefully pay attention to our embodiment, pure attention bare of expectation and purpose?

Paradoxically, the importance of our embodiment is being re-emphasised through theory and research. New discoveries should cause us to change long-held and fundamental ideas. Current research, as we have seen, reveals the indivisibility of body and mind. The division of the duality of body and mind is no longer tenable. We know now that processes of mind take place not just within the brain but also between brain and the rest of the body. Candace Pert, who undertook some of the fundamental research into the chemical bases for emotional process, has described the way that the immune system is interconnected with the endocrine and nervous systems, and how they are all joined to one another in a multidirectional network of communications linked by information carriers called neuropeptides (1997). Mind, one could say, is that which holds the network together. Thus we can say that mind is *embodied*. It is instantiated throughout the body in these molecules of information. In fact, Pert suggests a definition of mind as flow of information. As such it is non-material, non-physical, yet with a physical substrate which is both body and brain, conscious and unconscious, psyche and soma.

Many others, in different ways, have endorsed this reconnection of body and mind. The concept of man as machine, followed by that of mind as computer, for long guiding metaphors in science and cognitive science, are being challenged. The group of "enactive" neuroscientists such as the late Francisco Varela propose a similar understanding of embodiment and its inseparability from mind (1999).[1] He stated firmly that the mind is not in the head: cognition is embodied. It is a process brought about by action, by a moment-to-moment coping and coupling with the world such that what appears to be outside or objective and what seems to be inside or subjective cannot be separated.

In another recent book and television series, the neuroscientist Susan Greenfield also emphasised the integration of body and mind, stating that to model a brain in its entirety one needs also to model a body. Elsewhere, the same scientist suggests another definition for the term "mind": that it should be used to describe the personalization of the brain, the way that certain configurations of neuronal connections individualise each brain (2000, pp. 13–14). Each brain becomes individually configured in accordance with individual experience. Such individual differences, she suggests, should be called "mind". Thus, importantly, she brings together mind and self. If mind is seen as divorced from body, our idea of our self will be different from the idea we will have if mind and body are seen as indivisible. Seeing them thus, body may become the lived foundation of our experience rather than a possession or part of our (self) image.

Despite the fact that these theoretical findings challenge the split of mental and material, and the location of the confirmation of our existence in our thoughts, the Cartesian credo "I think, therefore I am" still profoundly colours our expectations and our experience, and forms a "default" mode arising from earlier understanding. The error of this was suggested by the philosopher Ludwig Wittgenstein, who wrote: "One of the most dangerous of ideas for a philosopher is, oddly enough, that we think with our heads or in our heads. The idea of thinking as a process in the head, in a completely enclosed space, gives him something occult" (1967, p. 605).

Practically too, through the development of ever more sophisticated means of transport, heating and communication, over the past few centuries life for most people has become increasingly distanced from physical work and from involvement in the natural world and the turning of the seasons. To become warm today, for example, usually involves the mere pressing of a switch rather than hours outside the house, chopping and carrying firewood. Simultaneously the power of image has been continually strengthened through the development of means of communication, first printing, then television, film, and computers to a current extreme manifested in the very term *virtual reality*. All of this has fostered a progressive and, I would suggest, damaging movement away from valuing and paying attention to our embodiment, and an ever-growing movement towards abstraction and the power of the image. By continuing to think in our heads and valuing thought and mind above body, we have come to identify with our thoughts.

Such dangers have been noted. Joseph Campbell thought that "the body has become a victim of its own imaging process gone haywire" (Keleman, 1999, p. 20). By identifying only with the image rather than with the embodied experience, we become decentred, not only alienated from much of our own experience but also reliant upon the other as the viewer of our image. In the words of another writer: "The fault of Narcissus is not that he loved himself but that he loved his image in the eyes of others" (Norretranders, 1998, p. 321). Take the fashion for exercise: today it is commonly recommended and practised less as an acknowledgement of the needs of the body lived from within than in the service of the image, the shape of the body in the eyes of others.

In his most recent book, the third of a trilogy dealing with new trends in neuroscience, the neuroscientist Antonio Damasio continues the restoration of the importance of body. He emphasises once again the impossibility and non-viability of separating it from mind, insisting that they form an integrated organism, interacting fully and mutually, through chemical and neural pathways. He writes of the "body-mindedness" of the mind, saying that it, the mind, only exists because there is a body to present it with content; the images that occur in the mind are reflections of the interactions between organism and environment. He points out that considering mind in the perspective of the body, as compared to considering it merely in the perspective of the brain, supplies us with a rationale for mind that we could not discover through consideration only in terms of mind alone. "The mind," he states, "exists for the body, is engaged in telling the story of the body's multifarious events, and uses that story to optimise the life of the organism" (2003, p. 206). The mapping of body states is fundamental to the processing of emotion, while presentations of the internal state integrated with external or internal stimuli form the basis for our experience of the world.

Findings from this research of the "second generation" of mind scientists has also given support to a new approach to philosophy, "embodied realism", which attempts to realign many of our deeply rooted ways of thinking in accordance with these new discoveries. The main proponents of this new philosophy, George Lakoff and Mark Johnston, describe the shifts we have mentioned (1999). Reason, they state, can no longer be considered as disembodied and transcendent, but arises from the very nature of brains, bodies and bodily experience. Thus it is also evolutionary, building upon rather than transcending our animal nature. Reason is not, then, some essence that distinguishes us from other animals, rather it situates humankind on a continuum with them. They also insist that reason is not dissociated from emotion but is always inevitably emotionally engaged. Moreover, they too emphasise that it is only the tip of the iceberg of rational process that is conscious, most of the process lies below consciousness. Yet the sense of embodiment is centrally important also to the higher levels of consciousness, those that we consider most specifically human. Lakoff and Johnston's particular addition to this argument is the belief that reason is not literal but works in a metaphorical and imaginative manner.

Fascinating earlier research by Lakoff and Johnston has shown how language is embodied, formed from the imaginative and metaphoric extension of basic primary metaphors that themselves arise from our very sense of embodied being (1980). This metaphoric conceptual system is utterly embodied. It is initially founded upon our physical experience and built up by a process of neural selection. The primary metaphors are acquired just by our normal moving and perceiving in the world. As a domain of subjective experience is co-activated regularly with a sensorimotor domain, permanent neural connections are established. These basic sensorimotor concepts are literal, but the primary metaphors occur when a concept from a source domain (the sensorimotor domain) is imaginatively extended to apply to another target domain (the domain of subjective experience). We can take concepts of spatial relations as an example of this. Spatial relations concepts make sense of space for us. We perceive an entity as *in, on, along from, up, down,* etc. Metaphorically we extend this embodied, sensory spatial experience to the subjective valuing domain: for example *good* is *up, bad* is *down;* prices rise and fall; we aspire upwards and fall downwards both actually and morally. Lakoff and Johnston have identified many other primary metaphor schemas such as those of container and contained, and source-path-goal schema.

Even abstract concepts from love to morality and causation may be conceptualised via multiple and complex metaphors. Each complex metaphor will be based upon primary metaphors. Each primary metaphor is embodied in three ways: through our experience of the world which pairs sensorimotor experience with subjective affective and evaluative experience, through the neurally instantiated logic of perception and motor movement, and through the neural instantiation of frequent co-activations. All this is largely unconscious and beyond conscious control; it is part of the undermind, the cognitive unconscious.

Such new discoveries upset the traditional distinctions of conscious-unconscious and body-mind, even person-world and especially literal-imaginative, showing boundaries to be far more fluid and our logic perhaps far more "fuzzy" than we have recently considered. This has implications for psychotherapy, which has always operated in the domain of the unconscious—which we now see is an even larger domain than previously thought. As we have seen before, Allan Schore suggests that the dynamic unconscious is represented by right brain processes, and that right brain to right brain intersubjective transactions lie at the heart of both infant development and the reparative therapeutic relationship. To speak generally, for all such interactions are immensely complex, the right brain is primarily involved in embodied rather than linguistic information. Thus he has suggested that psychoanalysis should be called the "communicating" rather than the "talking" cure (2004). Such extended communication involves the body. As noted in Chapter Three, Freud had written: "The Ego is ultimately derived from bodily sensations" (1923, p. 16). However, he had not followed up this line of investigation. To engage in this, the therapist must be able to access her own bodily-based intuitive responses to the clients' implicit bodily-based communications. She must learn awareness of posture, gesture, and energetic messages. New approaches are needed that question commonplace wisdom and return us to penetrating awareness of our experience, freed from the constraints of unchallenged philosophical dispositions such as the dualities of body-mind, reason-emotion and conscious-unconscious.

The Buddhist attitude towards embodiment has traditionally been different from that of the West. In the West we find a tradition of mind-body dualism, with some bias towards the mind as the stronger and more important part. In contrast, in the East there are many traditions which appear to understand their relationship better, and treat mind and body with far greater equality. This profound initial difference has important consequences. In particular, it has led to differences of approach to philosophy and practice. In the West the disciplines of philosophy and science, theory and practice have often developed separately, with science focusing on the physical world as external nature and ignoring the relationship between mind and world. It is interesting to note how European philosophy has been far more concerned with time and Japanese with space, the place of experience.[2] For Buddhism both philosophy and practice, as we have discussed, are founded upon human experience and concerned with all dimensions of such experience. Thus there are important differences in attitudes to training. The Western assumption is that training proceeds from mind to body, from belief to behaviour, while Eastern views of mind-body oneness are the foundation for methods of self-cultivation that affect, train and transform the mind through the body. A further difference is found in the relationship between theory and praxis: in the East praxis has usually taken priority over theory, while in the West it is usually the other way around.

Thus for Buddhists, body is the foundation of experience, and while it may lead us astray, without it liberation is not possible. *Samsara*, the Buddhist term for our ordinary human life of endless rebirth and suffering, is a Sanskrit term which refers to the tendency of life to go in circles, to repeat itself. The contemporary Buddhist writer Stephen Batchelor contrasts this with the idea of a path, which may lead forwards. He interprets samsara in a manner most complementary to today's scientific findings.

> The repetitive tendencies of samsara characterise existence itself. The forces of nature incline towards stable and predictable patterns: the circling of planets around the sun, the recurrence of the seasons, the phases of the moon, the ebb and flow of oceans, the unfurling of a bud into flower ... the replication of sequences of DNA. Samsara is not only a psychological process. Its machinations are at work in our chemistry and biology as much as in the repetitive obsessions of our psyche. [2004, p. 61]

The Buddha declared: "It is in this very fathom-long physical frame with its perceptions and mind that, I declare, lies the world, and the arising of the world, and the cessation of the world, and the path leading to the cessation of the world."[3] Later one of the great Tibetan writers and practitioners, Tsong Khapa, bases the legitimacy of conventional truth not, as one might expect, upon conventions of belief or theory but upon embodiment. "For the world whatever is apprehended by six unimpaired senses is considered true. Everything else stands as false for the world."[4]

The six senses, as we saw in the previous chapter, are those of the five senses of sight, sound, smell, taste and touch, plus the mental sense of cognition. Preliminaries for Tantric practices of Vajrayana Buddhism state repeatedly the necessity for appreciation of our human rebirth as the only foundation for gaining enlightenment.

Throughout the Dharma we find reference to the divisions of body, speech and mind. All these terms are somewhat wider than their common Western usage. The Buddhist conception of body embraces the mind-body continuum in its sense-based experience. Speech too refers to more than mere speech in the western idea of it, relating to communication, imagination and affect. Mind also embraces understanding and relationship with world. Loosely, one could say that they are reflected in my divisions of embodiment, emotion and environment.

The fourth noble truth, as we saw earlier, outlines the eightfold path leading to liberation. The seventh stage, right mindfulness, refers to practices of mindfulness of body, feelings, mind and phenomena. There are two major sutras, or discourses, that particularly relate to such practices of mindfulness.[5] Mindfulness of body starts with the breath, with conscious breathing, so mind and breath become one. Then, following the breath and breathing with awareness of the entire body, mind and body are brought into harmony. Through calming of the breath, mind and body are stilled. Awareness of body is practised in all positions and actions, and the parts of the body are contemplated and mindfully observed. Through observation of the four elements present in the body, the interrelationship of body with world is contemplated. This is followed by contemplation of impermanence.

Here we may find evidence for devaluation of the body, for the images suggest decay and putrefaction. Indeed there is so much variation within Buddhist teachings and texts that I could possibly have put forward an alternative argument in favour of Buddhist contempt for body as being the source of desire. This is too large a detour to engage in here, but one can distinguish different paths to liberation according to different approaches of Buddhist thought. Early Buddhism, based on the sutras, has frequently been described as the path of renunciation whereby ego and desires are overcome by rules and practice that lead to abandonment of unhealthy emotions. Later, in the Mahayana, more emphasis is placed upon the power of compassion and the understanding of emptiness to act as antidotes to ego and desire. The Tantric path of Vajrayana employs the path of transformation, using practices of energy and imagination to convert conventional experience into awakened experience. Finally the supreme way of Dzogs Chen offers the path of self liberation in a non-dual contemplation of the nature of mind, empty, clear and unimpeded, which is at the core of all.

In a contemporary commentary, Thich Nhat Hanh suggests seeing the verses that apparently devalue the body from a somewhat different perspective. Such contemplations, which he advises should only be practised by those in good mental and physical health, rather than teaching hatred of our bodies, should teach us to see how precious a human life is; that it should not be wasted, nor its impermanence ignored.

Attention is then directed to watching feelings as they arise as pleasant, unpleasant or neutral, and then it is directed to watching one's general mental state. Finally these three stages are integrated in contemplation of the totality of physical and mental processes, the world as it is displayed in the interplay of the groups of physical and mental events. In all these contemplations attention is drawn to change, to the coming-to-be and the cessation of the constituents that comprise the experience.

Through mindfully observing the coming and going of the processes of embodiment, teachings of impermanence, selflessness and interdependence can be realised directly. Understanding gained in this way has a different quality to cognitive knowledge or accumulation of facts, as is well experienced in psychotherapy. There is a subtle but definite distinction between thinking and embodying an idea. As a contemporary Buddhist writer has expressed it: "This ground mindfulness collapses the mind-body opposition ... suggesting the possibility of an *embodied* groundedness, one that takes its certainty and steadiness as much from a specific way of holding mind and body as from ideas or ideals" (Klein, 1995, p. 154; my emphasis).

In many other Buddhist texts we find acknowledgement of the conjoint importance and inseparability of mind and body. In a work which, tellingly, brings together philosophy, ritual and medical practice, a thirteenth century Tibetan writer proclaimed that even if the mind is understood with the greatest wisdom, one will never be fully enlightened until one understands the body.[6] In similar vein, in a contemporary magazine article a leading meditation teacher speaks of the Buddha as a super-scientist, stating, "If proper attention is not given to the sensations, then we are not going to the deepest levels of the mind. The deepest level of the mind, according to Buddha, is constantly in contact with bodily sensations. And you find this by experience."[7] Neuroscientists would agree. Through attention to sensations, one trains the mind to resist reacting non-consciously to them. It is interesting that this accords with the scientist Benjamin Libet's defence of free will despite his research which showed that preparation for action precedes consciousness of the impulse to act. He locates free will in the conscious power of veto: free won't rather than free will (1999, pp. 47–57). Such findings endorse the importance of the cultivation of mindfulness.

I wonder if attention can revalue our embodiment. So often we take our bodies for granted until such time as they give us trouble. Language itself encourages us to consider bodies as possessions as in that last statement. Such attention may also help us to see through the metaphors of language rather than accepting them literally and seeing ourselves as objects rather than processes. The task is to reinhabit our bodies, seeing them as the valued source of our experience, not as the mere possessions of a disembodied and transcendent mind or reason. The task is also to free language from the hand of dead metaphor, to reconnect with living imagination and with the newness of unknowing. It is to encourage a precise attention to experience as it actually occurs in every moment, rather than experiencing always through a filter of expectation, past experience and emotional colouring. Such an attention produces a different way of being rather than knowing. The difference between embodying an idea and thinking rests in a presence of attention, rather than in completeness of knowledge. It results in an embodied groundedness which finds steadiness and certainty from a way of being rather than from any beliefs and theories.

Attention to embodiment may be a blessing and resource in other ways. From the beginning of the twentieth century we have been, and are, faced with notions of the death of God, the cessation of the metamyths, the end of metaphysics, and the closure of "ontotheological" discourse. Against such deconstruction how can we find a foundation for ethical behaviour? If one commonly accepted Truth has given way to the views of many truths, how may we escape drowning in relativity? Amongst all this discourse, there is a small chorus of voices pointing to embodiment as a living *way* beyond such dead ends. Just as for animals living well is living naturally, so may we return to our embodiment as a source for our ethics. One writer writes of visceral coherence rather than narrative coherence as a way of making sense of our lives (Klein, 1995). Such coherence, not dependent on language, may lead us to a way of reconstruction beyond deconstruction and duality—to a lived conjunction of experience and meaning. Another speaks of a "vivial sense"—the "clear awareness of one's taste of life", a way of testing philosophic theory not dependent upon an abstract idea of truth (Sprung, 1994, p. viii). Yet another, Mark Johnston, mentioned earlier as a proponent of embodied realism, has written of the imaginative character of the moral understanding. He too suggests that embodiment and imagination may provide the foundation of a contemporary ethics, walking the middle path, free from either moral absolutism or moral relativity

(1995). Based on our processes of cognition and constrained by biological, social and linguistic interactions, all grounded in common human embodiment, a foundation for a common ethics may be discovered. The Dalai Lama bases his own "ethics for a new millennium" upon our capacity for empathy and compassion, an understanding that flows from our interdependence and shared humanity. As we will see in our discussion of selves, ideas of embodiment, of self and of ethics are closely interrelated.

Do we any longer pay attention, notice the different feel of carpet or pavement or new grass? Do we notice how the air feels before rain or after rain, how wind affects our emotions? Do we take time to ask ourselves how we feel after we have spent time walking, or running, or even in the gym? Do we allow a moment just to feel the air on our skin while we jog, the wetness of the water as we count our laps? Such attention to our embodiment leads us both in and out. It brings awareness to our selves as they change and move moment to moment, and to our interface with what is not us, with our environment and ourselves as embedded within it. It also teaches us the ultimate openness, contingency and emptiness of reality as it is, both rich and empty.

Breathe in
air from outside,
wind on face,
rustling as it moves through the leaves,
sun's warmth.
Breathe out
into world,
warm breath
utterly dependent upon
the next breath.

Sharp cold wind
as cloud circles the sun.

Just sitting
self shrinks,
body stays,
awareness clear,
empty,
full of world.

Notes

1. See also Appendix 1.
2. See the work of Nishida Kitaro and Watsuro Tetsuji. Also Yuaso Yuasa (1987, 1993) and Shigenori Nagatomo (1992).
3. *Samyutta Nikaya II*, 3.6. An excellent exposition of this story by Andrew Olendzki, "This fathom-long carcase", appeared in *Tricycle*, Spring 2005.
4. Tsong Khapa, *rTsa she tik chen rigs pa'i rgya mtsho*, p. 408, quoting from *Madhymakavatara*.
5. *Satipatthana Sutra* (found in both *Majjhima Nikaya 10*, p.145 and *Digha Nikaya 22*, p. 335) and *Anapanasati Sutra* (*Samyutta Nikaya II*, p. 1516). Both these sutras have been translated with contemporary commentaries by Thich Nhat Hanh as *Transformation and Healing* and *The Sutra on the Full Awareness of Breathing*.
6. *rGyal-ba Yang-dgon-pa rGyal-mtshan dpal* (1213–1258). I am indebted to Janet Gyatso for this quote, from a paper given at the IABS conference in Lausanne, 1999, and subsequent correspondence.
7. "Superscience", an interview with S. N. Goenka in *Tricycle*, Winter 2000.

CHAPTER SIX

Emotion

I feel I think, therefore I am.

(Broks, 2003, p. 100)

Knowing about emotion and feeling and their workings does matter to how we live.

(Damasio, 2003, p. 208)

She is sitting on a low couch, cross-legged, leaning back against plump cushions. Her hair is curly and a little wild around a small pretty face. A slim, lithe body is hidden under thick sweaters and bulky sweat pants. Her feet are tucked up under her. As so often when we have sat here weekly for the last year, she is telling me a story.
I listen to her story,
to her words,
to her body,
to the space between us,
and to my own response to all of this.
And I feel a disconnection, under the words a hesitation.
I wait a moment, the story continues,

she tries a smile, but the smile doesn't fit the words
—my feeling is stronger, and in a pause, I interrupt.
"Can you stop there for a moment?" I say.
"How is it for you now, telling me this?"
She pauses, knowing now how the work goes.
Her face squinches a little in inner focus, her eyes close.
"There's a heaviness," she says
then silence.

I wait.

She touches her belly. "I feel it here":
More silence
"It's kind of dark and heavy—and there's a small sharp edge—like
anxiety."
Silence again.
Her hand moves over her belly.
"Can you stay on that edge?" I ask.
"Its uncomfortable, but I'll try."
More silence, and the atmosphere in the room feels slow.
She shifts in her chair. "The edge is crumbling, it's like the anxiety is
softening, and I'm on the edge of the slow heaviness."
"How is that?"
"It's OK," she says.

More silence.

She swallows, and from her closed eyes the tears begin, but the air
feels lighter. Something has altered.
"I felt abandoned—I am still alone—but now it's bearable. I can bear
it—the weight is shifting a little."

I wait.

And she looks up, and smiles, and we are back in relationship again.
She begins to talk about the experience, to bring it back to story.

This is just a moment from a fictional therapy session. In a
contemplative psychotherapy, the movement goes between
story and feeling. The aim is to slow the story, dive beneath
the words to release the feeling. Often the core feeling is deeply buried
or layered; anger hiding fear; shame hiding grief. Slowly, by paying

attention to the feelings, acknowledging them without judgement, just letting them be, or—in the words of one writer—"befriending them", we peel away the onion skins. The mere acknowledgement of feelings in the sunlight of attention slowly unknots their charge, so that they may in time be re-written into a new narrative. Until acknowledgement is achieved, progress is impossible. A little like training a wild animal. First comes trust and kindness.

The body is a guide. We are attempting to touch into a level that is prelogical, preverbal, preconscious. The body gives us hints—the therapist will find her own body a guide to what she is picking up in the space. What is the client doing (saying) with his own body language? With pure attention therapist and client may meet in a preverbal place, a being to being meeting in a relational field. Neuroscience is using terms such as right-brain-to-right-brain syn-chrony and affective resonance to describe what occurs in early development between parent and infant, and it is a similar process that allows for healing in psychotherapy.

Neurological research shows the way emotional self-regulation develops during early interactions between parent and infant. Psy-chotherapy, often the repair of early damage, would seem to work best in much the same way. Relationship and trust between client and therapist creates a safe relational space in which (re)develop-ment can occur. Repressed and frightening feelings may be explored in a safe relationship, without judgement or consequence. Nor should we forget positive emotions. Research has shown that the shared experience of joy and play between parent and child plays an important part in development. Psychotherapy often has a tendency to overlook laughter and positive emotions, perhaps finding them inappropriate when the focus is so often on pain. This is demon-strated both by the name and the late arrival of the psychotherapeu-tic modality of Positive Psychology in the last years of the twentieth century. Some years earlier, the psychoanalyst Nina Coltart had written tellingly of the almost transgressive feelings she had when first allowing laughter in a session (1992, p. 12).

Recent Western research into emotion has led to a re-evaluation of both the constitution and the importance of emotion in human being. Earlier scientific interest concentrated upon knowledge and knowing, and cognitive reason was valued at the expense of embodiment and emotionality. Now the balance is starting to be redressed. It is telling that this field was initially entitled *cognitive* science. Now with both cognitive and affective neuroscience, a wider title is needed. Current research is uncovering both the centrality of embodiment and emotion and their inescapable participation in the constitution of cognition itself. Several recent books tell the story of this research and illustrate the discovery that focusing on intelligence without attention to affectivity leads to a very partial picture.[1]

As mentioned earlier, Candace Pert's work, described in *The Molecules of Emotion* (1997), outlines the chemical component of the story. She recapitulated the research and the personal journey that brought her to the discovery of the importance of embodiment and the centrality of emotion in our experience and our health. According to Pert, the neuropeptides and their receptors are the molecules of emotion that form the biochemical link between body and mind. She describes the manner in which those parts of the brain concerned with emotion, frontal lobes, amygdala and hippocampus, are extensively connected with immune system, endocrine system and hormone regulation, and the autonomic nervous system that regulates heart rate and blood pressure. In this manner mind influences body and mental states have an impact on physical health, demonstrating both the indivisibility of the two and that the traffic between body and mind is not merely one-way. Something happening in the body affects the emotions; equally, emotional activity affects somatic processes. Any change in physiological state is accompanied by change in "mental" emotional state and vice versa, whether conscious or unconscious. More importantly, as described by Pert, the free flow of the peptides brings the body and emotions to health. Physiologically the flow of emotion leads to health; if emotions are ignored or disassociated from, the flow is impoverished or blocked. A condition of stress causes and becomes an interruption in the flow, an information overload whereby sensory input, unprocessed due to suppression, dissociation or indigestion, inhibits free flow. As we have seen, continued stress during early development may both physiologically and psychologically disrupt normal development.

From the neurobiological perspective, Antonio Damasio presents a multi-branched model of emotions, starting evolutionarily with the most basic body-based metabolic regulations which support homeostasis, such as basic reflexes and immune responses, up through behaviours of pleasure and pain, drives and motivations, on to emotions, which he distinguishes into background emotions, primary emotions and social emotions. Background emotions he describes as being composite expressions of the regulatory behaviours of the lower levels, as they unfold and interact moment by moment in our experience, the result of which is our momentary "state of being". This state is that which we consult when asked "How are you?" and which we detect in others by the energy or expression or "vibes" they give off. Primary emotions he defines according to traditional groupings of emotions, such as fear, anger, disgust, surprise, sadness and happiness. Social emotions are those most dependent upon their social context, such as sympathy, embarrassment, shame guilt, contempt, etc. Above these occur the conscious experience of emotion he terms "feelings".[2] According to his current view, "feelings are the expression of human flourishing or human distress, as they occur in mind and body. Feelings are not a mere decoration added on to the emotions, something one might keep or discard. Feelings can be and often are *revelations* of the state of the life within the entire organism" (2003, p. 6). Here again we find both the indivisibility of mind and body, the centrality of the emotions in the flourishing of human life, and an acknowledgement of how much of these processes occurs below conscious awareness. In his current terminology, Damasio uses the term "emotions" as being aligned with body, feelings with mind.

According to Damasio, an emotion is a complex collection of chemical and neural responses that form a distinctive pattern. Such a pattern is produced by a normally functioning brain when it detects what he calls an emotionally competent stimulus (which we could liken to the sensorimotor contingencies central to the enactive approach in Mind Sciences, described in Appendix 1), which triggers an emotion. This response is automatic and engenders changes in the state of the body and the brain structures which map the body and support thinking. The result of these responses is to place the organism in circumstances favourable to survival and wellbeing — natural eudaimonia. As we saw above there is a hierarchy from non-conscious body-based affective response reactions to conscious feelings.

These theories have important implications for education and for psychotherapy's emotional tutorial. Emotions and feelings are central to the process of developing both brains and selves. Difficult early circumstances may result in an abnormally functioning brain, whereas good early modelling of emotional regulation enables us to respond effectively to circumstances and to understand that the higher, conscious responses can be modified to some extent. Feelings that embrace attention, imagination, reasoning and past memories enable us to respond to circumstances creatively and with some measure of wilful control. We can regulate our exposure to stimuli that arouse reactions; we can, with effort, learn to engage brakes on our reactions and resist or modify them to a greater or lesser extent. This is one of the key areas where neuroscience, psychotherapy and Buddhist practice may come into dialogue. As Damasio says, "One of the key purposes of our educational development is to interpose a non-automatic evaluative step between causative objects and emotional responses" (2003, p. 54). Research such as his is helping to uncover the molecular and cellular mechanisms necessary for emotional learning to occur. Damasio speaks of freedom as "a reduction of dependencies on the object-emotional needs that enslave us" (*ibid.*, p. 276). It sounds somewhat Buddhist. Indeed the definition of a destructive emotion in Buddhism is anything that clouds clear apprehension of reality, anything that disturbs equanimity. The task is the same whether it is described in Buddhist terms or in those of Spinoza and William James, of whom Damasio writes that their goal was the individual and inner task of restoring balance, the "homeodynamic balance that is lost as the result of anguish" (*ibid.*, p. 282).

Emotional tutorial helps to instil methods of tolerating and regulating feelings. It involves some form of modification of the automatic reaction and transformation into willed response. The first step is to acknowledge our feelings. Only through acknowledging them, bringing them to consciousness, making friends with them and integrating them into our life narratives can we restore flexibility and "flow" and put an end to repression and disassociation. To this end Buddhism may offer its two thousand years of awareness practices. Candace Pert suggested that meditation, by allowing long-buried thoughts and feelings to surface, may be a way of getting the peptides flowing again and so returning the body and the emotions to health (1997, p. 243). This also explains why meditation retreats can be psychologically challenging for meditators, and stir up unexpected feelings.

In her book *Human Minds,* the psychologist Margaret Donaldson also pointed to Buddhism as a valuable system of education in what she sees as one of the stages in the development of certain mental abilities which she calls the "value-sensing" or the affective faculty. Exploring the development of human minds, Donaldson was, unusually for that time, as concerned with the importance of emotional development as with intellectual development. She distinguishes between bodily sensational feelings and emotions, describing the latter as our value feelings: "They mark importance. We experience emotion only in regard to that which matters" (1992, p. 12). She states that this strand of development is one that has been overlooked and undervalued in the West, both in education and in research, and turns to Buddhism despite her own stated lack of knowledge in this field. Progressive development of value sensing modes supports an opening up of egocentric sense of self, the expression of which is compassion.

Contemporary accounts of embodied and affective cognition also involve intersubjectivity. Evan Thompson, a supporter of the "enactive" branch of cognitive science and a colleague of the late Francisco Varela, concludes that the affective mind is not in the head but in the whole body, and moreover is not only a whole organism event but also a two-organism or self-other event.[3] Such references to intersubjectivity are increasingly common and are found not only in neuroscience. To take a few examples, ideas of intersubjectivity occurred earlier in psychology in the work of the Russian psychologist Lev Vygotsky concerning what he termed "the zone of proximal development", where an infant learns and develops through the "loan" of the adult capabilities of his or her carers. Schore's study of development and attachment, as we saw, traces the path of emotional regulation from interpersonal regulation in the context of the mother-baby dyad to self-regulation. Similar ideas are also present in the theories of the analytic school of object relations theory. In philosophic fields these ideas appear in the work of Merleau-Ponty, Husserl, Patocka and the dialogism of Bakhtin.

Such teachings show that human minds develop only through intersubjective experience. Evan Thompson has suggested that empathy is to be understood as a unique and irreducible kind of intentionality which is the very precondition of consciousness, and which can only be formed in the dynamic interrelationship of self and other. Schore's research supports this, and he suggests that empathy is seen to be "the critical manifestation of the human experience, and relatedness and interactive regulation the desired end-state" (2003a). His work consistently underlines the centrality of intersubjectivity in development and in reparative healing, stating that the intersubjective field co-constructed by two individuals includes not just two minds but two bodies (*ibid.*). Such theories are scientifically supported by research into a class of neurones called the mirror neurones, which are found to display the same pattern of activity both when specific actions are carried out and when the same actions are observed being performed by another. Their discovery has led to interesting hypotheses as to their role in learning. Earlier, the psychologists Lacan and Winnicott both used the term "mirroring" metaphorically to describe the process whereby a mother attunes to her child's world and gives shape to her needs.[4] This mirroring gives form to the disorganized processes of the infant, and makes them part of one relational process until such time as they are able to separate out from their environment and form a self; a self that has been created in response to this reflection. In Winnicott's words:

When I look, I am seen, so I exist,
I can now afford to look and see. [1971, p. 114]

When adequate reflection is not forthcoming, one can see the damage to the infant. Psychotherapy offers this same mirroring as a means of repair. Empathy and affectivity are essential to development, and we are determined by our relationships with others and with our world.

Emotions regulate what we experience as reality. What sensory information travels to our brains and what is filtered out depends on the signal receptors are receiving from the neuropeptides, the molecules of information and emotion. The nervous system, scanning the external world, interprets it according to its own integral capabilities, its developed patterns and its past experience: an interpretation that, as we have seen, fits well with ancient Buddhist models.

As we have also seen, emotions are central to social responses, and thus play a critical role in ethical behaviour. Damasio quotes approvingly from Spinoza's *Ethics*: "... the very first foundation of virtue is the endeavour (*conatum*) to preserve the individual self, and happiness consists in the human capacity to preserve its self."[5] Damasio adds that the secondary foundation of virtue, which inevitably follows on from this due to the fact that our inalienable need to maintain ourselves and be happy necessitates the preservation of other selves, "is the reality of a social structure and the presence of other living organisms in a complex system of interdependence with our own organism" (2003, p. 171). He finds in this the foundation for a system of ethical behaviours which is neurobiological, based on the observation of human nature rather than religious revelation. According to this, "good objects are those that prompt, in reliable and sustainable fashion, the states of joy that Spinoza sees as enhancing the power and freedom of an action. Evil objects are those that elicit the opposite result" (ibid., p. 172). Good actions are not merely those which accord with individual appetites and emotions, but are necessarily those which do not harm other individuals. This accords well with the Dalai Lama's definition quoted earlier, that "genuine happiness is characterized by inner peace and arises in the context of our relationships with others." Both are attempts to base a system of ethics on a real appreciation of our human nature, which as we learn is both interdependent and intersubjective.

For both Buddhism and Taoism, ethical behaviour rests upon a foundation of seeing clearly and acting dispassionately. From the Buddhist perspective, as noted earlier, the very definition of a destructive or unhealthy emotion is "something that prevents the mind from ascertaining reality as it is" (Goleman, 2003, p. 75). Seeing clearly entails not projecting our fears and desires onto the world. Unclouded by our fears and desires, we may see the situation for what it is, and act appropriately. Hence the Buddhist project of attention: first we bring awareness to our afflictive mind states, and then we attempt to remove afflictive emotions and strengthen healthy ones.

There are two main areas for the espousal of Buddhist practices of mind training. That of most concern for academic Western science is in the field of research. Research into consciousness, as noted earlier, needs to be able to work from different viewpoints, paying attention to the phenomenological level as well as the neurological level. Further research into the area must take account of experience. Yet science lacks the mental disciplines reliably and repeatedly to access specific subjective experience and to distinguish subtle emotions.

Experienced meditators have through long practice acquired deep familiarity with their own mental life, and can discriminate very subtle differentiations between feelings, and show a disciplined ability to access such specific and subtle mind states at will. The research now taking place at Madison, Wisconsin under the neuroscientist Richard Davidson is exploring these areas.[6]

The second area is more important for psychotherapy and for most of us in our daily living. The intention of Buddhist mind training is transformation. There is an oft-repeated story about the Buddha and a man shot with an arrow. What is the need, the Buddha is reported to have said, of questioning where the arrow came from and why, rather let us look to how we may heal the wound. Sophisticated and thorough practices of attention are, as William James noted, central to emotional education. Research by Damasio and others has shown that emotionally competent stimuli affect our organism whether or not we are aware of them. Though such research shows that these processes are to a large extent determined and non-conscious, yet there is space for some choice if our physical equipment is undamaged, and even for later repair of early damage. If we can bring attention and thought to them, practice in attention fosters greater awareness and greater veto. This building up of connection between an action and its emotional consequence requires a certain degree of integrity of the prefrontal region of the brain and may be beyond the reach of those who have suffered severe damage to the frontal lobes of the brain. Such damage has been found to affect emotional response to social stimuli to such an extent that normal emotional responses such as embarrassment, guilt etc. are simply unable to arise (Goleman, 2003, p. 61). However, with normal brain functioning, our responses may be exaggerated or ameliorated by cultural conditioning and conscious practices such as meditation and mindfulness. Of interest to both personal and research projects, current studies have shown that experienced meditators display vastly greater neural activity in those areas of the left pre-frontal cortex of the brain which are known to be associated with feelings of wellbeing than is found in the brains of control groups.

Meditation, rather than being actually included in psychotherapy as a distinct practice, may be of profound benefit for psychotherapy as a way of working with the emotions, for the therapist in training and in practice as well as for the client. The task of psychotherapy is to help the individual acknowledge and ultimately to accept *all* the depth and breadth of their experience. Emotional tutorial becomes necessary when an individual becomes stuck, identifying their being with only a part of their potential and of their experience. Often this is induced by past history. I ignore that part of my experience which is incompatible with what I see as the path to happiness. If I believe (having been taught early to believe) that if I think or feel a certain way I will be unlovable in the eyes of those whose care I depend upon, I will not be able to own that part of my experience. I will have to deny it, as that will be preferable to the risk of losing the love I need. I will then learn to disown that part of my experience, those unacceptable thoughts or feelings. Alternatively, I may have been told so often that I am "the stupid one" or "the sensitive one" that all my experience is filtered through this core belief, and experiences that would show me as "intelligent" or "insensitively strong" will be denied or reinterpreted. It will be hard for me to be any different way. The work in psychotherapy is so often first to identify our own identifications, then to take time to explore their limitations, while allowing and acknowledging our ongoing experience outside this framework. Culturally we have been encouraged to identify our-selves only with the conscious rational part: individually the con-striction is often worse, to identify only with the part that "fits" with the expectations of our early caregivers.

Buddhist meditation teaches a way of witnessing mental life, allowing and receiving but not reacting. The most essential part of the training of therapists is that they should be aware of and comfort-able with their own ongoing experiential process. They must know where the difficult areas are for them, so that they clearly recognise their own issues and prevent them overflowing into their clients' stories. Only by learning to be comfortable with one's own emotions can a therapist offer that comfort, safety and potential healing to a client. If a therapist is still frightened of, say anger, then the client's anger will not be welcomed. This is an example of the relational field effect in close dyadic process. Meditation practice allows the trainee therapist a method and space for learning to befriend emotions.

For the client a general attitude of mindfulness is helpful. While such practices as using breath as a focusing point to come back into present embodied awareness are useful, I personally feel that formal meditation practice is best kept entirely separate from the therapeutic journey. If clients in personal psychotherapy wish to meditate, their meditation practice should be taught by a meditation teacher and not by their therapist, thus keeping transference issues clear.

However, the way of mindful attention to what is arising in the moment is, I believe, at the very heart of good psychotherapeutic practice, as touched upon in the vignette at the head of the chapter.[7] By staying in mindfulness with the mind state itself, and not allowing our conditioned reaction, which is to shift immediately from the feeling itself into elaborations of the story surrounding it and the people involved in its arising, we can observe the state itself with mindfulness and attention. This is often termed "bare attention". More precisely, it is attention to the bare feeling, to the very anger or joy or disquiet itself, divorced for a while from its story and other emotions such as guilt, justification or judgement, which we frequently build upon that first feeling. It should also be divorced from identification with the feeling. The very fact of acknowledging the core state, witnessing it without identifying with it, allows the emotion to calm down and will ultimately allow it to transform. The Buddhist teacher Thich Nhat Hanh has written most clearly and helpfully of mindfulness practices. He writes: "Our mindfulness has the same function as the light of the sun. If we shine the light of our full awareness steadily on our state of mind, that state of mind will transform into something better" (1990, p. 86).

In this way the whole therapeutic encounter may be conducted in a meditative manner. Conducting therapy within the "witness" state provides a way of being for a therapist and a client. Early on Freud wrote of the necessity to suspend the critical faculty during psychoanalysis, encouraging analysts to suspend judgement and give impartial attention to everything there is to observe, advocating a state of evenly suspended attention. Activity is left behind, focused attention gives way to a softer, wider state of consciousness in which more features appear: the distinction perhaps between seeing through a telephoto and a wide angle lens. Such a state of attention will be familiar to meditators. We might even describe the method of a meditatively aware therapy as an alternation between the two forms of concentrative and analytic insight meditation, as the client is encouraged to move between stabilization upon a feeling, staying with the feeling and fully experiencing it, and reflecting upon it.

In all these different contexts, the central focus is on *being with* the arising mind state, of allowing it and witnessing it, but not *identifying* with it; to see it as arising and ceasing, as a transient component or facet of the self-process rather than as a permanent essential self. This different way of being substitutes depth of attention for completeness of knowledge as an aim, thus evading identification and closure. It proffers a different way of knowing, embodied, affective, and non-discursive. It refrains from imposing a finished self into world, leaving open space for change, potential and other.

I should also mention here modalities in which mindfulness is used explicitly as a practice in therapy. Jon Kabat Zinn has most successfully initiated the use of mindfulness practices, stripped from their "religious" or Buddhist trappings, to help in the management of stress and chronic pain. Building from his work, a form of therapy called Mindfulness-Based Cognitive Therapy has been found to be of great use in the prevention of relapse in patients who have experienced severe depression. In both these cases the presentation is overt and educational, and the patients enrol for a series of meetings with homework in between, in which they are encouraged through the practice of mindfulness exercises to experience a new way of knowing and of relating to their bodies, their feelings and ultimately also their thoughts.[8]

If these practices are of such benefit to psychotherapy, one must ask if psychotherapy itself is necessary; if Buddhism alone is not enough. Indeed, this is a question often asked within Buddhist communities, many of which are opposed to psychotherapy. My defence of psychotherapy is to turn to the intention of both practices. Buddhist practice has always presupposed a healthy individual, and is concerned with a wider liberation, even if it may be interpreted as liberation *within* the world, rather than liberation *from* the world. Psychotherapy is fully concerned with our conventional existence within the world. While the practices of Buddhist meditation provide a wonderful way of being with and befriending our emotions, the concern of Buddhism is with the way our mind works rather than with the contents of mind. Practitioners are often discouraged from spending the time which may be psychotherapeutically necessary with those contents. The method is the same: to note, acknowledge and let go of our mind states. However, sometimes we need both encouragement and "permission" to spend a little longer with difficult states before we are ready or able to let them go. The very practice of meditation will almost inevitably tap into emotional states, but meditators may not be encouraged to focus their meditative practices of attention onto these emotional mind states, "letting them go" long before, on a personal level, sufficient attention and acceptance have been achieved. It is important not to miss the specific on the path towards the general: to use the spiritual in order to ignore the personal. Such "spiritual bypassing", as it has been termed, sees concern with personal issues as beneath the concern of the spiritual seeker, and may confuse states of pre-personal fusion with those of transpersonal awareness. While Buddhism offers superb methods for psychological as well as spiritual health, the intention of Buddhists often overlooks the conventional realm. Sometimes also to explore previously unacknowledged emotions may be frightening, and we need the support and accompaniment of a therapist in this journey. This is the field of psychotherapy. As we have seen, recent research emphasizes the importance of relationship for emotional learning. It is particularly important today, when spiritual teachers are not part of a community with ongoing and daily knowledge of their students, but often jet in for talks to many, personally unknown listeners.

Psychotherapy has much to offer here. It has also much to bring to the understanding of the dynamics of teacher, student and group relationships. Its understanding of pathology, transference and unconscious processes can help the development of Buddhism in the West. A strict transfer of traditional methods from other cultures with different social and cultural norms and expectations into our contemporary Western context without sufficient awareness of these underlying factors has already led to many sorry scenarios in different communities. In embracing other systems of thought it is not wise to throw away our own heritage. As Buddha said, we should test according to our own experience. Equally, to interpret Buddhism as psychotherapy is to belittle its enterprise, to try to subsume the greater into the lesser.

Inextricably part of all our experience, emotions are inseparable from cognition. They influence our attention at the most primary levels of our interaction with the world and shape our very self-process. As the importance and centrality of emotions becomes ever more obvious, "emotional tutorial" becomes ever more necessary. Hopefully the work of those scientists and writers like Daniel

Goleman, who has led the crusade for emotional literacy, may make it less necessary, as generations grow up whose education has paid attention to affective as well as cognitive development. Consideration of our embodiment led to consideration of emotion, which must now take the leap beyond individual body-mind into our environment, both physical and cultural, to explore our situatedness.

Notes

1. For example: Goleman (1995), Damasio (1994), Pert (1997), Ekman & Davidson (1994).
2. Confusingly, we must be aware that Damasio uses the term "feelings" in a different way to which the term is used both in Buddhist models and also in the work of other neuroscientists.
3. See various papers in E. Thompson (Ed.), "Between Ourselves. Second-Person Issues in the Study of Consciousness", *Journal of Consciousness Studies* 8: 5/7, 2001.
4. Interestingly Lacan writes about an actual occurrence of vision in a mirror, rather than intersubjective reflection in the mother's gaze, and sees this mirroring as a *méconnaissance*, a false belief in organization and single alienating identity, "which will mark with its rigid structure the subject's entire development". See "The Mirror Stage", in *Écrits*, p. 4.
5. Spinoza, Proposition 18 in Part IV of *The Ethics*, as quoted by Damasio (2003, p. 170).
6. For up to date information on this and other projects, and for information about the series of meetings, see www.mindandlife.com and Appendix 2 below.
7. What is described here is much influenced by what might be termed a Western psychotherapeutic form of mindfulness, presented by Eugene Gendlin and called Focusing. This technique was based upon Gendlin's observation of clients who used psychotherapy well. It is now allied with many different forms of therapy. See Gendlin (1981 & 1996).
8. See Kabat Zinn (1990 & 1994). Also Segal, Williams & Teasdale (2002). Also Appendix 2.

CHAPTER SEVEN

Environment

I had no sense of size, sitting here. No distance or time. Not one thing could be separated or compared to another to give me a vantage. The stone, the horizon, my body, these could not be broken down any farther. My life had given me moments here and there, flashes of awareness upon the sudden passing of birds, upon an enchanting quality of light, or the upclose stare of a mountain lion, but never such sustained awakening as this.

(Childs, 2002, p. 212)

No man is an island, entire of itself; every man is a piece of the Continent, a part of the main; if a clod be washed away by the sea, Europe is the less, as well as if a promontory were, as well as if a manor of thy friends or of thine own were; any man's death diminishes me, because I am involved in Mankind...

(Donne, *Meditation* XVII)

I see sun shining on a pond, water moving with the wind, which is blowing through wind chimes hanging from the eaves. It is spring.

The air is filled with birdsong, solo voices close by in the bushes around the pond, chorus more distant all around the valley up again to individual cries of buzzards hanging and gliding high above in the air.

I hear the liquid call of a moorhen whose nest, constructed out of last year's bulrush stalks, I know is hidden among the kingcup leaves, concealed between their large green plates. Six eggs inside. As I watch, the female paddles out into open water, skimming and picking, picking and floating. Sound of splash as the picking beak trawls for weeds.

From some angles against the light I can see a small cloud of midges circling over the surface of the water. A white-orange butterfly skips by in jerking flight. The grass is starred with white daisies opening to the sun. Amongst the daisies are little mounds of bare earth.

It is spring; the leaves of the shrubs and trees are just beginning to sprout. Some are quite well unfurled; others are brown-edged, shrivelled evidence of the unseasonable cold snap just passed whose frost damaged their brief appearance. Yet others are still bare.

As I watch, there is a sudden explosion, an irruption in the surface of the water, and a deep glug sound. It's over too fast to see anything but there must be something down there, breaking the surface to catch a fly. I wait and watch. As I move towards the pond's edge, my presence betrayed by my shadow, I see another shadow slide over the pond floor: a large fish glides to hide under the weed.

The burnt leaves tell of the frost, the little earth eruptions on the grass tell of the presence of moles. Thousands of different stories, thousands of different life cycles in this small space. From the human perspective most of these are invisible, under the water, in the air, or taking place after dark. Each fragment is linked to every other in some way. As I sit by the pond, I hear the water trickling out into the old stone drainage channels that once lay under this water meadow which for over twenty years has been my garden. It was only after we had had the big earthmover in to dig the pond in the field, and let it fill with water from a pipe upstream, and flow out through another pipe back to the stream lower down, that we found these channels from an earlier history of the land. Water flowed in and water flowed out successfully, the level maintained correctly, until one morning when we found the level had dropped several inches below the outfall pipe. Where was the water going? We found it then, as now, by its sound: a sound of flowing water where none should have been. We discovered a channel by the side of the pond through which water was escaping. Moles tunnelling under the earth by the side of the water open up new outflows from the pond into the old subterranean drainage channels time and time again.

This sound of the water speaks to me of two of the many worlds of whose shadowy existence I am little aware, separated by time and space. The first is that of history, my own and all those who have come before me to this valley. Particularly in England, where the history of human settlement is long and space is limited, we occupy the same plot where many have been before us, leaving marks like the stone channels used to flood the water meadows to keep the land frost free and ready to provide good early grass. Such marks tell the tales of earlier farmers, as do the hedges and plantations.

In front of me across the pond is a beautiful old stone font which came, I believe, from a church in Italy. It was brought back from her travels by an old lady who lived in a small house far east of here in southern England. Later my parents bought her cottage, built on to it and lived there for fifty years. When they came to live in the South West, they prepared to leave the font as they had found it. I persuaded them not to leave it behind, and asked for it for the garden I was setting up. Luckily so, as I later learned that the new owner of their house swiftly sold the garden for two additional building plots. Thus, sitting here, listening to the water, looking up and seeing the stone font, I am connected over time to my family, to earlier farmers of this valley, to Italian churchgoers, and to an unknown old lady who lived by the sea and cared enough for something beautiful to go to extraordinary lengths to bring it home.

The second world of which the flowing water sings is that of the underground, the world of the moles that open up the channel, inhabiting a different lifeworld to us. They leave their marks on the surface; their hills and holes mark their presence by a negation, a lack of their actual appearing, only signs pointing to presence elsewhere. Under the earth, feeding on worms and insects, live the myriad denizens of a lifeworld we humans rarely catch sight of. Somewhat shocked, we occasionally find their miniature worlds when we overturn a log or stone, revealing a large toad that blinks and jumps for the water or the shade, while tiny beetles crawl and worms wriggle away from the light.

And under the water there is yet another world. I know that large fish, even an eel inhabit the pond, but I rarely see them. Even now myriads of water boatmen glide on or above the shiny surface of the water. Each patch of weed is another tiny universe sustaining micro-cosmic forms of life, linked together in an ecological web. Tadpoles, water beetles, newts, frogs and toads are but the larger and more easily recognisable characters in this aqueous world.

And above the glassy surface of the water is air. Just above the water cloud-like gnats hang and hover in shifting mists. Individual dam-selflies, red, electric blue and deep green, dash over the surface, and more solitary still, huge dragonflies with striped bodies and opal wings clicking as they catch the ferns and bulrushes in their flight. Higher still, the little birds swoop and flutter amongst the shrubs. On the pond itself the moorhens live, the young like miniature black feather dusters, the parents fussing, their white tail feathers leading the way into the safety of the rushes whenever a human approaches, their red beaks dipping and dabbing into the water as they feed when peaceful. Crashing from the higher trees around the pond the valley thugs, noisy pigeons, break the stillness. Higher still, buzzards drift in the upper air. From the woods on the slopes, as the light fades, the calling of owls echoes through the valley as another world enacts its own scenario, the world of the night dwellers.

After dark, another whole cast of characters takes over and occupies the world that humans dominate during daylight hours. As we retreat inside our artificially lit shelters or, if outside, congregate together with light and noise, around the edges of our awareness, many non-human actors take over the stage and go about their business, eating, playing, hunting and mating. In the morning only a few traces, legible to those fewer and fewer folk who know how to read them, betray what happened in the night.

Rabbits come out at dusk into the upper world, around the hedge lines. Badgers come out of their sets; sometimes surprised in the lanes, they barrel along in front of the cars, searching for an open gateway. Foxes slink along tracks and lope across the dark fields. A cry from a taken rabbit, the howl of a vixen in heat, the remains of an unfinished meal, the empty chicken run are all that tell of their passing.

Ultimately, if I can sit quietly enough and long enough, a transformation may occur in my relationship with all of this. Writing of the great Japanese Buddhist teacher and poet Dogen, Steven Heine points to this: "The observer must cast off his or her status as a spectator and become fully immersed in the unfolding of impermanence" (1997, p. 51). All these worlds share our environment. Yet we so rarely acknowledge them, or even accept that we share the world with them. Rather, we tend to see both the world and its non-human inhabitants as resources for our human desires. It has taken a long time for Western people to regain a knowledge never lost by civilisations more closely and less anthropocentrically linked to their environment, a knowledge of the interconnectedness of all life, a knowledge of human dependence as well as human power. Following the mechanistic and dualistic ways of thinking that have dominated modern science, nature has been seen as devoid of consciousness, objectified and independent of our perceptual experience of it (Wallace, 2002, p. 123). Newer disciplines and approaches contest this. Discussing neuroscience, we saw that enactive cognitive science challenges our normal divisions of brain-body-world. I also noted that Damasio described how he was led to answers for questions posed by consciousness only after he began seeing the problem of consciousness in terms not of the subject alone but of two key players, organism and object, and the relationship between them. Another contemporary discipline, ecology, with its holistic understanding, is a particularly modern Western discourse, though it is of course a scientific restatement of a truth intimately known by traditional societies. As we have lost personal connection with such lived knowledge, it has to be restated as theory.

Cultural psychology and ecopsychology are other bodies of theory which are concerned with human being in, and inseparable from, the environment. In the words of a recent book (Benson, 2001, p. 4): "Self functions primarily as a locative system, a means of reference and orientation in worlds of space-time (perceptual worlds) and in worlds of meaning and place-time (cultural worlds)." This writer, Ciaran Benson, understands self as an ongoing, dynamic process of location. Such an understanding recognises the centrality both of embodiment and of social relations. Cultural psychology has grown out of cognitive psychology, the movement that first brought consciousness and cognition back into the field of legitimate research. Divorcing itself from computationalism, with its guiding metaphor of mind as computer and its interest in information processing, cultural psychology focuses upon experiential human being and meaning-making. It is particularly interested in such processes as narrative, interpretation and dialogue. Like Buddhism, cultural psychology sees freedom not as a given but as a consequence of skills one has developed, which in turn depend upon beliefs and commitments which compose one's identity.

To bring such theories to life, however, we also need experience and emotional engagement—love in its widest sense—to enable us as particular participants to integrate with our environment in its particularity. We need to expand our awareness of our personal embodiment to awareness of its implication within the larger ecology. We need to re-engage with practice and particularity in a move away from abstraction and generality. Wendell Berry reminds us:

> My own experience has shown me that it is possible to live in and attentively study the same small place decade after decade, and find that it ceaselessly evades and exceeds comprehension. There is nothing that it can be reduced to, because "it" is always, and not predictably, changing. It is never the same two days running, and the better one pays attention, the more aware one becomes of these differences. Living and working in the place day by day, one is continuously revising one's knowledge of it, continuously being surprised by it and in error about it. And even if the place stayed the same, one would be getting older and growing in memory and experience, and would need for that reason alone to work from revision to revision. [2000, p. 139]

Revision equals re-vision, seeing anew. As we become more connected to our embodiment and to our emotions, so we may become more connected to our environment. Following upon the discovery of the inseparability of mind, body and emotion, we find the inseparability of individual and world. As world touches body, providing sensory stimulation, awareness of body and its boundaries may lead us to awareness of their permeability, to awareness of how embedded we are in the world. For in noticing ourselves we notice our limits, and becoming aware of our boundaries, we see that they are more permeable than we thought. In awareness of my skin, I become aware of the wind. Aware of the wind, I feel it on my skin. Aware of my self and my thoughts, I become aware of my relationships. To regain connection, we have to re-inhabit theory. Re-visioning environment requires implication. In place of the dispassion of scientific objectivity, it calls for compassion, involvement and care.

Such capacities of understanding are not only dependent upon our embodied structures and our emotions; they are also experienced and nourished within a world. Perhaps we should say: worlds. For this involves overlapping domains—the physical world, the world of intersubjectivity, and the world of culture and consensus. The research which suggests that sensory and motor processes, perception and action are inseparable is also teaching us the importance of context in development. Our earliest and closest environment is our family. As we have seen, individual experiences linked to specific environmental contexts play an important role in the development of the brain, which constructs itself through spontaneously generated and experience-dependent activity rather than through building up a collection of pre-specified modules. Affective interaction of self and other in infancy modifies the very constitution of the living tissue. Self is inseparable from other.

The neurological reinterpretation of attachment and developmental theory and the discovery of mirror neurons demonstrate in scientific terms that maturation is an intersubjective process. A baby alone will not become what we would recognise as a "normal" adult. Shared process and communication between infant and caregiver are part of everyone's development. Resonance, synchrony and affective transactions with other brains are necessary components of natural development. Previous paradigms using the model of the isolated brain are now seen to be inadequate to describe the process of development or, indeed, the process of repair. Intraspychic models are not adequate: interpersonal ones are certainly necessary. As yet one can only speculate about the transpersonal. Paradoxically, understanding of intersubjectivity gives a foundation for a theoretical, even a dispassionate understanding of compassion. If we are all interdependent, it behoves each one of us to feel with or for the others. But compassion cannot be dispassionate. It is active, action taken in the understanding that we are all interconnected; it is a fearless openness to what is other, in the knowledge that at base, there is no "other".

Connection and lack of connection, as healing and as problem, are strong contemporary themes. As they set the scene in early family life for future development, so they may also colour our later years. A psychiatrist writes of how in a big hospital he was frequently asked by other colleagues to prescribe anti-depressant drugs for elderly patients returning home from various kinds of surgery. When their files appeared on his desk for the prescriptions, in place of the expected drugs he would add his recommendations:

> As far as her depression is concerned, the best thing for this patient would be to get a dog (a small one, obviously, to minimize the risk of a fall). If the patient considers that would be too much work, a cat would do, since it does not need to be taken out. And if a cat still seems too much, a bird or a fish. Finally, if the patient still refuses, then a houseplant.

After many irritated responses from the other doctors, he prepared a document which summed up all the scientific studies endorsing the value of care and connection, proving that a loving relationship is in itself a physiological benefit (Servan-Schreiber, 2004, p. 180).[1] Whilst as far as he was aware, his colleagues never did fill his prescriptions as written, at least they ceased their derision of his ideas. His story shows how resistant the scientific and medical world has been to accepting new ideas that show how vital, if invisible, our emotional connections are to our health and wellbeing.

As so many of our lives become estranged from the natural world, the mental and symbolic cultural worlds we inhabit become ever more important, and the world of social and cultural convention becomes the primary world in which we live. In an earlier chapter we looked at the way language evolves through the use of metaphor, beginning in our experience of embodiment. As metaphors become embedded in the language, we forget their symbolic quality. They become dead metaphors, become understood literally. The writer Wendell Berry (2000) writes tellingly of the way language has evolved from metaphor through equation to identification. Here lies a danger. Buddhism calls it the danger of grasping, the cause of suffering. Buddhism points to four main types of clinging or attachment: attachment not only to sensual pleasure but also to views, to rules and observances, and to the doctrine of the self (*Majjhima Nikaya 9.34*). The last three are surely the pillars of our mental environment. It is our unfortunate habit to see our views, our beliefs and our selves as solid, real and permanent rather than as symbolic, processual and changeable. When we identify with these solidified selves, beliefs and views, suffering arises. What we need is a sense of participation, not of identification. However, as we are afraid of the unknown, identification appeals to our egocentric search for control and certainty. Participation asks for a much humbler and braver exocentric attitude of implication. The distinction between compassion and pity illustrates this. Pity is something I may feel for something other than myself; compassion is suffering with, feeling with something from which I am not separate.

The world that Buddhism has explored for so many centuries is one in which the power of mind in the construction of world has never been doubted. In contrast, in the West we have long followed the objective path of representation, seeing our experience of the world as a re-presentation of a pre-given world, a world that is independent of the knower. Paradoxically, this has made our own view of ourselves both more arrogant and more bereft. As we saw, following the dictates of science, nature has come to be seen as devoid of consciousness, both objectified and independent of our perceptual experience of it (Wallace, 2002, p. 123). At the same time as this has occurred on a theoretical level, our lifestyles, with escalating urbanisation and technological advances, have increasingly removed us from meaningful engagement with nature at a physical and practical level. These two movements have left us out of balance.

As we saw when discussing the view from neuroscience, there are a small but hopefully ever-more influential number of cognitive scientists moving towards a different, non-representational or "enactive" stance. From the perspectives of Western science and philosophy, they propose that mind and world are mutually dependent. Mind is there to make a world. As we have seen, the central insight of this orientation is the view that cognition is embodied, and that knowledge and experience are the result of ongoing interpretation that emerges from our embodied capacities of understanding through sensorimotor coupling. Perception, according to this view, is obviously central not only to how we see the world but, to a greater extent than formerly understood, to how we create it. For example, scientific research proves that colour does not adhere in things, nor is it an essence in and of itself, but it arises from interplay of circumstance and processes within and beyond the seer: what Buddhism has long called dependent co-arising (Varela, Thompson & Rosch, 1991, p. 149).

How we see the world influences how we live in it. These views utterly challenge our conventional divisions of inner and outer, self and other, subjective and objective. Such views could uphold another "middle way", one between unobtainable objectivity or realism and utterly relative subjectivity or idealism. The concern of such enactive approaches to perception is not to recover the comforting security of a perceiver-independent world but to find and understand the linkages between sensory and motor systems that will teach us how action can be perceptually guided in a perceiver-dependent world (*ibid*.). The message of such views is a reconnection of organism and environment as bound together in reciprocal process. It presents a picture of dependent co-emergence and intersubjectivity and the inseparability of seer and seen that may well be more compatible with the Buddhist philosophy of non-duality than that of scientific materialism.

Perhaps these views may help us to rebalance our view of self and environment, even man and environment. It may encourage us to see what is there for its own sake, not for what use it can be to us. A twentieth century philosopher wrote: "It is not *how* things are in the world that is mystical, but *that* it exists" (Wittgenstein, 1921, 6.44). In thirteenth century Japan, Dogen had described the desired balance:

> To practise and confirm all things by conveying one's self to them is illusion; for all things to advance forward and practise and confirm the self is enlightenment... To learn the Buddha Way is to learn one's own self. To learn one's own self is to forget one's self. To forget one's self is to be confirmed by all dharmas. [*Genjokoan*, Abe & Waddell, 2002, p. 133]

Such a perspective informed Basho's exhortation:

> From the pine tree
> learn of the pine tree
> And from the bamboo
> of the bamboo.

Mindfulness can bring us back to the lived particularity of our environment if we can experience it from a position of embodiment and passionate engagement. It always seems so sad, when hiking in glorious country where there is so much to wonder at, to stand aside on a narrow trail as runners come by, eyes fixed, hands clenched, earphones clamped over ears. With sweat dripping, they are out to conquer both body and environment, senses shut down, inward, open only to their own chosen and controlled environment, closed to all that is other. The potential of the earth to invoke wonder, to heal our small and circumscribed experience, is ignored. It sometimes seems an appropriate image for the way we all too frequently inhabit our bodies and the earth as instruments of our will.

As I sit by my pond, I am enworlded—not only in the physical world, but also in the world of my culture. I can only make sense of what I see according to my experience, my education and the cultural world of which I am a part. The sight and sounds of spring would have a different meaning were I a working farmer. My pleasure in the birdlife would be different were I a professional zoologist; again quite different were I a hunter. My history, sharing that of the water channels and the old lady traveller, is that of a southern English-woman. To this has been added study and reading in other cultures in which I have travelled. Implicit in my understanding and my enjoyment of these different lifeworlds is my own cultural environment and my own emotional development. It is a continuing task to bring awareness to my own experience and also to the cultural and emotional filters through which I experience it. Such awareness can help re-vision these environments, in turn transforming future experience.

Above all, we need to find new images to enable a new way of appreciating our implication in the world, rather than seeing it as just a mechanism or a background for our human activities. Ecofeminists and deep ecologists have put forward the idea of world as active agent rather than passive backdrop for human life, or potential resource, or threat to our cherished sense of self. Donna Haraway, resisting the appeal to a primal mother and acknowledging all the symbolic and psychological baggage that motherhood and femininity carries with it, writes of "coyote knowledge", stating that to acknowledge the agency of the world in knowledge makes room for some unsettling possibilities, including a recognition of the world's independent sense of humour. The coyote, a trickster figure from Southwest Native American mythology, "suggests our situation when we give up mastery but keep searching for fidelity, knowing all the while we will be hoodwinked" (Haraway, 1991, p. 199). This may not lead us to comfort, but it does preserve us from the seduction of false consolation. To lay down control, identification and egocentricity, or even anthropocentricity, acknowledgement of the trickster, would help us to concede our uncontrolling participation in both the physical and the symbolic worlds. Let us see how humble yet engaged attention to embodiment, emotion and environment may help us re-vision our selves.

Note

1. A long list of studies proving that love is a "biological need" and the benefits of relationship for health and wellbeing is to be found in the notes to Chapter 11 of his book.

CHAPTER EIGHT

Selves and non selves: I, mine and views of self

In its widest possible sense, however, a man's self is the sum total of all that he CAN call his, not only his body and his psychic powers, but his clothes and his house, his wife and children, his ancestors and friends, his reputation, his works, his land and horse, and yacht and bank account.

(James, 1890/1981, p. 291)

A major challenge for neuroscience in the twenty-first century will be to try to figure out how brains and selves go together.

(Broks, 2003, p. 52)

Here and gone. That's what it is to be human, I think—to be both someone and no one at once, to hold a particular identity in the world (our names, our places of origin, our family and affectionate ties) and to feel that solid set of ties also capable of dissolution, slipping away, as we become moments of attention.

(Doty, 2001, p. 67)

Were mind and matter me,
I would come and go like them.
If I were something else,
They would say nothing about me.

(S. Batchelor, 2000, p. 114)

So, then it's the one
who has thrown his self away
who is thought the loser?
But he who cannot lose self
is the one who is really lost.

(Saigyo)

I sit quietly by the pond,
Take a deep breath
And bring my attention to my body.

In this moment of calm before the busy day begins, I turn my attention to the way I feel.
As attention moves from body to feeling to mind, it moves out and engages with world.
Sitting by the pond, I draw together all the stories that surround it, like a spider,
with my self at the centre of the web, filaments extending in all directions, radiating outward, bringing nourishment and form back. Like a spider, I have woven this web and the web has formed me.

The ripples begin to move outward with my gaze.
Feelings and memories flood in, bringing colour and story.
I look outward onto my home.
My sight and memory engage—the trees I planted so long since that now they soar above, cutting off the sun, causing the faint shadow that makes me suddenly chill—all the plants and objects so carefully chosen over the years.
I remember my children hunting for Easter eggs around the old font, and think of them now in their adult lives. Still further out my mind leaves its home ground,
into the world,
into all the situations and selves that the day will bring,
different kinds of work, friends from different worlds, each of which reflect back a different image of myself.

Back into past, forward into future,
I travel through time and space as
Self ripples outward,
wider and wider from the body sitting on the step by the pond.

I (subject) feel (verb) body (object).
"I feel I think, therefore I am."
Body, feeling, thoughts inseparable.
Seamless happing —
Coloured by feeling,
Divided up by language.

The I that looks
is made up by the looking,
the feeling, the embodied process,
the stories and the possessions it looks out upon,
divided up by living,
body, feelings, possession and memory
weave in and out of the valley,
dance over the water like dragonflies
in summer, woven together
like reflections on the surface of the water
that receive trees and sky
and offer them back.

So this garden, my most intimate place, reflects the self I feel closest
to me, and yet I know that in another place the kaleidoscopic pieces
of selfing would settle another way, reflecting other aspects —
aspects of self chosen like dress to suit the day. And still I say "I",
as one, and feel I as one, forgetting changes of time and place and
memory, even as I feel that I am not myself this morning after a
night of restless sleep. Even as I speak of my body as a possession
of some more inner I.

It is an intimate mystery that I live every moment, weaving together
and looking out from all these facets of self as intimate to my feeling
of who I am as my body.

Breathe in
Breathe out,
Mind and body brought together in breath
Even as eyes engage with world.

E verything discussed in the preceding chapters should have changed our attitudes, and most importantly our feelings, towards our selves. It has hopefully shown that our "selves" emerge "in process" from the experience of our embodiment, our emotionality and our environment of family, culture, nurture and nature. Yet still, day by day, we consider our "self" as an existing "thing" rather than as an ongoing process. Our selves remain things until in their interaction with world they cause us obvious pain. Buddhism has long understood both a different conception of self and the very importance of this for liberation from suffering. The idea of no self is one of the most central teachings in Buddhism; it is also for Westerners one of the least understood and the most difficult to grasp. Yet, as we have seen, even the most cursory survey of contemporary Western discourse reveals views of self coming from many directions which, carefully considered, may not be so very different. They reveal a picture of selves that under examination lose their definition and singularity while retaining their power of action. Antonio Damasio has suggested that a sense of self is an indispensable part of consciousness (1999, p. 7). So what is the self? And what is it not? What does Buddhism deny? What does the West assert? Are there any comparisons between the two that can usefully be made?

Let us begin with terminology. We are confronted not only with different conceptions of self but also with similar ideas expressed in different terms. One man's ego is another man's self.[1] The immediate response to the conception of self, I think, is usually—or perhaps until very recently has been—that which the philosopher Charles Taylor has called the "punctual self", the point of self-awareness in abstraction, in isolation from its constitutive concerns. It is that self which John Locke described when he wrote: "We must consider what Person stands for; which, I think, is a thinking intelligent Being, that has reason and reflection, and can consider it self as it self, the same thinking thing in different times and places."[2] However, if we look more closely and follow recent studies we find, even in the West, a sense of self that is not a thing but a construct, and one that appears to be considered as ever more widely distributed. William James was one of the first to consider this, spreading the sense of self over body, mind, possessions, family, society and reputation.

Since then, much has been written and discussed cognitively about the deconstruction of self and phenomena: science, psychology and art have revealed the self to be as insubstantial as Buddhism has, but to differing effect. Such knowledge has led too often to nihilism, to despair and emptiness, and a concurrent urge to fill this emptiness with material or even ideal consumption. As Buddhism engages with all aspects of our experience, cognition, emotion and physicality, its teachings state that construction of an erroneous belief in self comes about through a threefold process, emphasizing instinctual, affective and intellectual aspects in the form of conceit, craving and views of self. Conceit manifests in the linguistic form "this I am"; craving occurs in the linguistic form "mine"; and views of self are manifested in the form "this is myself" (*Samyutta Nikaya*). Western disciplines may now have come to terms intellectually with views of self, but would seem singularly to have failed affectively with conceit and craving. As the singularity and permanence of the "I" has been deconstructed by psychology, art and cognitive science in the West, it has been accompanied by an ever-increasing compensatory grasping of possession (consumption) and egocentrism (conceit) to fill the perceived gap.

The shadow side of our increasing individualism is lack of self-esteem, a common theme in Western psychotherapeutic circles. This is the view of emptiness merely as lack. Knowledge of contingency has not been accompanied by understanding of the positive aspects of interdependence and emptiness, or by a concern with the emotional implications of such knowledge. Tibetan Buddhism emphasises strongly the necessity for all enterprise to rest upon the twin pillars of wisdom and compassion. Without compassion, wisdom becomes only cognition and theory, which has too often been the sole support for Western discourse. Compassion in its fullest sense refers not to some kind of care for others but also to implication and connection: com passio = I feel with. It implies resonance, interdependence and intersubjectivity. Most importantly, along with the neglect of emotion, the theory of Western science and philosophy has been divorced from personal, experiential practice. We have lacked the practices developed by Buddhism, firstly to expose our normal (default) ways of seeing and being, and secondly to transform them. The understanding that our normal view of ourselves is erroneous is not just a fact or piece of knowledge for Buddhist teaching. The purpose of discovering this error through careful observation of our experience is so that we may transform it and alleviate our suffering. The philosophy and psychology of Buddhism are there to underpin practices which may enable us to develop clear sight and compassion, and to instantiate them in our daily lives.

Buddhist view of non-self

As we have noted, the third of the three marks of existence relating to all dharmas, alongside impermanence and suffering, is *anatta* (Pali: non-self), and the concept of selflessness is one of the distinguishing characteristics of Buddhism. Yet when we look at the life of the Buddha Sakyamuni, we see a man who possessed personal continuity, identity and personality. What then is the self that is to be rejected, and what is it that Buddhism denies? The Tibetan dGe lugs pa tradition makes a distinction between the "mere self", the transactional self which functions conventionally in the world, and an absolute or essential self, a fictitious self which is to be denied.[3] Let us revisit a few of the Buddhist models we have already discussed.

Buddhism provides us with maps of mind and of self, which show how our central ignorance of the way selves and worlds really arise colours all our lives. The central Buddhist map of self shows the coming together of five psychosomatic processes or aggregates: form, feelings, perceptions, dispositions and consciousness. Form refers to the physical basis of our existence. Feelings encompass those first feelings that draw us towards something, or push us away, or leave us indifferent, upon which more fully articulated emotions rest. It is interesting to note that a contemporary Western scientist also discriminates between emotions on this same basis. Richard Davidson postulates approach-avoidance as a fundamental dimension in distinguishing between emotions (Ekman & Davidson, 1994, p. 413). It is on the foundation of these primal and mostly unconscious affective pulls and pushes—attraction, repulsion and indifference—firstly that our attention is directed, and secondly that developed value judgements arise.

Perception refers to the processes of apperception and conception, the recognition of what one experiences. Psychotherapists writing of development have noticed that early emotion is very much about drawing people closer or pushing them away. Such early interpersonal experience becomes organized into schema of perception. In turn what is repeatedly perceived becomes an expectation. Expectations help the baby predict what may happen next and how to respond. Such expectations clearly relate to the fourth skandha, dispositions.

This fourth process, dispositions, is the most complex and difficult to translate and explain. Other translations for this are formations, mental formation, intention and volitions. This is the aggregate of our intentions and dispositions which accrue from previous experience and expectation, whether we see this as the mark left by actual earlier lifetimes (as traditional Buddhism would have us believe) or by previous experience in this one. These dispositions dispose us to react to subsequent experience in a certain way, feeding back into all subsequent experience in the form of emotional colourings such as expectation, fear, hope, shame and so on. As we have noted, earlier research has shown that this, our very subjective experience, can become mental *formation*, becoming neurologically instantiated, leaving discoverable traces at the neurological level.[4]

Antonio Damasio writes a neurobiological description of Spinoza's term *conatus*, or endeavour, in terms that could not but remind one of this fourth skandha: "It is the aggregate of dispositions laid down in brain circuitry that, once engaged by internal and environmental conditions, seeks both survival and well-being" (2003, p. 36). Even the terms "aggregate" and "dispositions" are those commonly used to translate the Sanskrit terms *skandha* and *samskara*. In a discussion by a contemporary writer on the neuroscientific foundations of psychotherapy, we find a description which might well apply to this aggregate: "Our hidden layers present to us a picture of the world with an agenda based on what has worked in the past" (Cozolino, 2002, p. 161). This agenda, with its perceptual biases and distortions, may be individual, arising from our own experience, or shared, with seemingly genetic evolutionary origins such as fear of spiders or snakes.

It is with this fourth component of the selfing process that psychotherapy is centrally concerned. Much of psychotherapeutic work is to do with disidentification, with loosening tightly grasped identity to allow for change, growth and creativity. The more we identify with the past, with what we *have* been, the harder it is to change what we *may* be. Through awareness of our (pre)dispositions, and encouragement to reveal them and make friends with them, we may open up some space for reflection and choice rather than automatic reaction. Our personal histories, whatever their stories, show a progression from dispositions to fixations which become obstacles. The flow of experience becomes an obstacle course around the fixations we have erected, often all-unconsciously. One of the most popular of Buddhist sutras, the Heart Sutra states:

> The bodhisattvas, grounded in the perfect understanding
> Find no obstacles for their minds;
> Having no obstacles, they overcome fear
> Liberating themselves forever from illusion
> And realizing perfect nirvana.

Free from the fixations we impose on the pure flow of experience, there are no obstacles, no self-images to defend, no fear of attack for nothing substantial exists to be attacked—total liberation. This is described by a Western scientist: "You lose—really lose the psychic, intellectual, emotional visceral sense of your egocentric self. That coincides with a complete loss of all the visceral ingredients that must underlie our sense of fear."[5] Some forms of Buddhism, notably Zen and Tibetan rDzogs chen emphasise the importance of spontaneity and naturalness, unfettered by fixations.

All of these processes are accompanied by the fifth aggregate, consciousness. Buddhism distinguishes six forms of consciousness relating to its model of six sense organs. Adding to the five senses distinguished in the West is a sixth, or mental consciousness. In this model Buddhism displays equal emphasis upon processes of body and mind, and their inseparability. This model emphasises the reciprocal interdependence of all five aggregates. It is easy to see how our first feelings affect our attention, then our perception, and how these develop our dispositions, which then influence all our subsequent feelings and perceptions. Just imagine how different we feel as we leave our house to go out when the sun is shining and the air is warm, and on a bitterly cold, rainy day. Just imagine how we feel as we see a large dog approaching, when we remember a similar dog bit us in our childhood.

Our experience of our "self" arises from the interplay of these processes. However, rather than viewing ourselves as an ongoing process, we tend to hold our selves as existing as some ghost in the machine, some permanent partless ontological entity. From the Buddhist point of view, due to basic ignorance of the interdependent nature of these aggregates and all phenomena, this process of selfing, this dynamic experience of ever-changing process, is grasped at as an entity, as some kind of container of the ongoing experience, and identified with. In contrast, in mindful awareness we can become aware of the rising and falling, coming and going of the discontinuous thoughts, perceptions, feelings and sensations which make up what we like to imagine as a single coherent and continuous self. This has been beautifully described:

> This arising and subsiding, emerging and decay, is just that emptiness of self in the aggregate of experience. In other words, the very fact that the aggregates are full of experience is the same as the fact that they are empty of self. If there were a solid, really existing self hidden in or behind the aggregates, its unchangeableness would prevent any experience from occurring; its static nature would make the constant arising and subsiding of experience come to a screeching halt. [Varela, Thompson & Rosch, 1991, p. 80]

So in ordinary experience it is the identification and appropriation of these experiential processes by an allegedly solid sense of self that causes the suffering of *samsara*. The five aggregates or heaps of process become solidified into what are termed the five aggregates of grasping (*upadana skandha*). It is interesting to note again that grasping or clinging is traditionally classified into four types: clinging to pleasure, to views, to religious observance and to belief in self (*Majjhima Nikaya*, 9.34). Without such grasping, one could perhaps aspire to the purity of perception suggested in Buddha's teachings to Bahiya in the *Udana*:

> In the seen there will just be the seen; in the heard, just the heard; in the reflected, just the reflected; in the cognized, just the cognized. This is how, Bahiya, you must train yourself. Now Bahiya, when in the seen there will be to you just the seen, then, Bahiya, you will not identify with it. When you will not identify yourself with it, you will not locate yourself therein. When you do not locate yourself therein, it follows that you will have no "here" or "beyond" or "midway-between" and this would be the end of suffering. [*Udana* 10.8]

Buddhist descriptions are descriptions of process, of how things are rather than what they are. So how does the sense of self come about? In the twelvefold description of dependent origination (*pratityasamutpada*) relating to the development of suffering human life, the same factors or aggregates appear in a different order. We are shown a cognitive cause in the form of basic ignorance (1) of the three characteristics of existence: impermanence, unsatisfactoriness and lack of essential self; from which arise the mental tendencies or dispositions (2); consciousness (3); and name and form (nama rupa) the collective term for the five aggregates, (4), which include and repeat both dispositions and consciousness, respectively the fourth and fifth aggregates; and the six senses (5). Then from contact (6), and feelings (7), that first unconscious evaluative act of going towards, avoidance or indifference, we meet the affective cause, craving (8), then grasping or addiction (9), which give rise in turn to being in delusion—what Buddhism calls *samsara*—(10), birth (11), and ageing and death (12). This is the cycle of suffering relating to human life. We can note that there are overlaps within and between these models. Whether this is just the result of oral transmission or the earliest description of what we would today call feedback loops, I shall leave open. Clinging to some aspects of experience, rejecting and denying others, grasping at an ever more solidified sense of self, which increasingly has to be defended, leads to suffering.

In another description, the Buddha said that name was comprised of the five factors of intention (*cetana*), attention (*manasikara*), perception (*samjna*), stimulation or contact (*sparsa*) and feeling (*vedana*). These same five factors were presented as the five constant factors of consciousness in the Theravada Abhidharma, the earliest systemisations of Buddhist psychology, and in a later presentation by Asanga in the Mahayana. Thus they are the foundation for a working sense of self. Here we can see a forerunner of contemporary descriptions of the close interplay between feeling, attention and sense of self. The illusory self with its concomitant egoic grasping is a superimposition resulting primarily from ignorance, reinforced by the naming process of language, which conceives of this fluid transactional self as permanent, partless and autonomous. Once one grasps, clings to and identifies with a permanent, partless self-concept, the pride and craving adhering to this become the pivot from which an egocentric world arises.

The self, then, which in Buddhism is to be negated, is an illusion. It never exists in the fashion we consider it to do. It is the imposition of a container self, with attributes of independence and permanence, upon the foundation of the conventional, transactional and "mere" self that is a process of ever-changing body-mind states, the interaction of self-processes.

Central to this progression of expansion and solidification is something called in Sanskrit *prapanca*, often translated as conceptual proliferation. It is another difficult term to translate, and entire books have been devoted to the subject, such is its importance. The major locus for discussion of *prapanca* rests upon a passage describing the development of visual awareness:

> Dependent on the eye and forms, eye-consciousness arises. The meeting of the three is contact. With contact as condition there is feeling. What one feels, that one perceives. What one perceives, that one thinks about. What one thinks about, that one mentally proliferates. With what one has mentally proliferated as the source, perceptions and notions tinged by mental proliferation beset a man with respect to past, future and present forms cognizable through the eye.
> [*Madhupinkika Sutta* of *Majjhima Nikaya*]

This description clearly shows how mental proliferation arises, and how in turn, in circular fashion, it influences all subsequent cognition.

Some commentators[6] point to the idea of separateness that adheres to the term *prapanca*, implying, in fact, an erroneous imposition of separateness upon things that are really dependently originated. The most important attribution of separate independent existence is that to the self. The pivotal separation is the statement "I am" from which all further attributions of separateness spring. As the Buddha taught in *Sutta Nipata* 916: "The wise man should put a stop to the thought 'I am', which is the root of all naming in terms of manifoldness." In psychotherapeutic terms, I have heard a contemporary Tibetan Buddhist teacher refer to this separation of the sense of self as the primary projection.[7] To continue putting this in psychotherapeutic terms, we first project a separated self upon the connected processes of being, and then we repress all awareness of having done this, and take our separated selves and the world "out there" for objective reality. The Buddhist writer Santideva suggested a different way of seeing ourselves:

In the same way as the hands and so forth
Are regarded as limbs of the body,
Likewise why are embodied creatures
Not regarded as limbs of life? [In: Batchelor, 1979]

This is the reason that Buddhist thought is so concerned with self and its deconstruction. As we noted earlier, there is no hard division in Buddhist teachings between psychology, ethics and practice. Buddhism is fundamentally concerned with finding out how the mind works in order to see how it may be transformed to operate more healthily and happily. Conceptions of self form the focus for self-cherishing and the initial separation from others and world. Described in neurological and contemporary terms: "Because we see a complex world from a single vantage point, our perception has an inherent egocentric bias. Our egocentric bias leads us to believe that everyone who sees the world differently is simply wrong or mis-guided" (Cozolino, 2002, p. 162).

Buddhist philosophy of dependent origination and emptiness pro-vides theory and meditation provides practices whereby we can first learn to recognise the fabricated and impermanent nature of the self, and then train ourselves to expand our self-concern over a greater area. The importance of this is echoed in contemporary terms by Daniel Dennet, who describes how by making oneself small, one can externalise the causes of one's actions and deny responsibility. The more responsibil-ity is externalised, the less the compassion. He says that through the evolution of communication, culture and education humans can work against the selfish gene, opening up a world of imagination and possi-bilities of transformation. He speaks of the "human capacity to rethink one's *summum bonum* as the possibility of extending the domain of the self" (2003, p. 180). We can see here how closely ideas of self are inter-linked with concepts of responsibility and ethics. A fully realised dis-tribution of one's sense of self evolves into a homeostasis that spreads out beyond the isolated and defended self to include the realisation of compassion in its true meaning of "feeling with".

Some Western views of self

Turning to Western views on the development of consciousness and selfhood, which appear to be inextricably intertwined, we find many descriptions of self process. Descriptions of both phylogenetic and individual development of a sense of self distinguish between the development of a working sense of self or continuity and that of a self concept which develops on top of this. Briefly, in the development both of the species and of the individual, bodily awareness comes first. This is followed by representation of one's own physical state, a move from self-monitoring to self awareness, which leads to the imputation of a self onto system. As we have seen, in human development these early processes are carried forward in a dyadic development "borrowing" the capacities of the early caregiver. Once this imputation of self onto system is symbolised within language, it is reinforced and reified by the social structures and value systems of the cultural sphere. Self image as process retaining a connectedness with environment gives way to self concept, which becomes increasingly solid and autonomous. Almost all models demonstrate some kind of development from some form of minimum self or immediate self awareness to some form of narrative self, a coherent concept extending back into the past and forward into the future.

Many models also show this two-tier development from transactional self as process to self concept reinforced by language and culture.[8] We see this distinction between a transactional self and a self concept that tends to become solidified, a distinction between an ever-changing experiential response to the environment, and the concept of a reified continuous self living in an objective world that is not so far from the Buddhist perspective. Indeed, another Western philosopher, Owen Flanagan, has written of the "apparent accident that Buddhism, almost alone among the great ethical and metaphysical traditions, holds to a picture of persons that is uniquely suited to the way science says we ought to see our selves and our place in the world" (2002, p. 208). What we have learned about the brain so far supports the idea that consciousness or self does not arise from any single region or neural network, but from interaction. They are complex functions constructed from multiple neural networks which are mostly non-conscious. This interaction is not only internal but also external—between individual and other, individual and world.

An interesting recent view of the construction of self from neuroscience is that of Antonio Damasio. As noted earlier, Damasio says that a path towards a possible answer to questions posed by the self only came "after I began seeing the problem of consciousness in terms of two key players, the organism and the object, and in terms of the relationship those players hold in the course of their natural inter-actions" (1999, p. 19). Emotions, according to Damasio, are central to the development of "selves", and, in circular fashion once again, something like a sense of self is necessary to make the signals that constitute the feeling of an emotion known to the organism having that feeling (*ibid.*, p. 8). As the brain creates mental patterns for an object, the brain also engenders a sense of self in the act of knowing. Consciousness, according to Damasio, is the unified mental pattern which brings together object and self, and which rests upon largely non-conscious foundations of response and attention.

Damasio's model describes the development of the self through the stages of *proto self, core self* and *autobiographical self*. Develop-ment begins with proto self, which is a coherent, but non-conscious collection of neural patterns mapping, moment to moment, the state of the physical structure of the organism. This is not located in any one place and is a product of the interaction of neurochemical signals between a set of regions. Above the level of consciousness the core self occurs as the feeling that arises in the representation of the non-conscious proto self as it is in the very process of being modified. Beyond this transient core self triggered by any object, the autobiographical self arises, dependent upon autobiographical memories, constituted by repeated instances of individual experi-ence. Damasio describes different levels of consciousness: core con-sciousness is the process of achieving a neural and mental pattern, bringing together instantaneously a pattern for a presenting object, a pattern for the organism, and a pattern for the relationship between these two. Extended consciousness occurs when working memory simultaneously holds both a particular object and the autobiographical self.

Each development of self shows a widening of the area of self: proto self is a map of the current representation of the organism, core self adds a feeling of the protagonist of this representation, and autobiographical self is able to extend backwards into past accumu-lated memory and forwards into a future anticipated in dependence on the past based upon dispositional records of core self experiences. Autobiographical self grows continuously with life experience and can be remodelled, at least partially, to reflect new experiences. Thus the hope implicit in neuroplasticity and Buddhist practice for this autobiographical self is under cultural rather than genomic control. Practice may transform, at a deep level. It may allow us to bring conscious attention to previously automatic process.

Self and identity, as we have seen, develop from self experienced in relationship, familial and cultural. Culture and language are factors we must not ignore in consideration of selves. Language structure, to a greater or lesser extent in different languages, fosters the understanding of the separated self as the subject of actions. Differences in cultural conditioning are profound and have a powerful effect on ideas of self, emotions and ethics. This is particularly demonstrated in relation to the independent self highly valued in the individualistic West, and the interdependent self more typical of Asian cultures, Once again this demonstrates how closely these fields—self, emotion and values—are related.

Turning to psychotherapy, we find many different models of self development, which share the characteristic that they all see self as a compound and a construct. Freudian models delineate conscious, preconscious and unconscious and ego, id and superego. Object relations theory sees the development of self occurring through interaction with others. Attachment theory seeks to centre psychoanalysis on early attachment rather than Freud's Oedipal model. Neuroscience is endorsing this view, showing that both physically and psychologically, early attachment experience impacts upon the organisation of the right brain, and that selves are experience-dependent.

Perhaps one can say that different schools of psychotherapy (analytic, humanistic and transpersonal) see the image of the self as covering a wider area: intra-, inter- and trans-personal. Jack Engler, who has written most perceptively about the oft-perceived difference between Buddhism and psychoanalysis in their approach to the self or ego, speaks of both as viewing self as a representation "which is actually being constructed anew from moment to moment" (1984). From this perspective the task is to acquire a cohesive functioning sense of self and to acknowledge it as a construct (both self and non self), and to be aware that the self is a construct and that to remain healthy it needs to be reconstructed from moment to moment. Our suffering and psychological ill-health arise from identifying with a permanent self concept, grasping it and seeing our life and world through the lens of this concept, refusing to move with change and impermanence.

However, in actuality I believe that psychotherapies themselves often lose touch with acknowledging the self as a construct. Attempting to heal the defective self image, or replace an inappropriate with a more appropriate one, they forget in the process that any self concept is just that: a concept, and that close identification with that concept, however appropriate, will ultimately be unhealthy and unhelpful in a changing world. The "true" self is ultimately only another screen for being, just as much as the false self. Only Lacan in Western psychology outside the contemplative therapies seems to see the image of the self as a whole as a *méconnaissance*, as not only a construct but, in the way we relate to it, a false one. Outside psychology such understanding is also rare, but Thomas Merton, writing in his journal, beautifully described this seduction of the "true self":

> The time has probably come to go back on all that I have said about one's "true self," etc., etc. And show that there is after all no hidden mysterious "real self" OTHER THAN or "hiding behind" the self that one is, but what all the thinking does is to observe what is there or objectify it and thus falsify it. The "real self" is not an object, but I have betrayed it by seeming to promise a possibility of knowing it somewhere, sometimes as a reward for astuteness, fidelity, and a quick-witted ability to stay one jump ahead of reality. [1997, p. 95]

Just as current scientific views of the development of the self appear to have taken us quite a way from any unitary, essential and "punctual" view, in the worlds of theory and art too we follow the modern and postmodern shadow of the vanishing subject. This may take many different forms, but in all cases a substantial representation of the self at the centre of its world is replaced with a more relational and distributed concept of subjectivity, and a more contingent one. As the philosopher Charles Taylor pointed out, citing Merleau Ponty, Michael Polanyi, Heidegger and the later Wittgenstein, much of the most insightful philosophy of the twentieth century has gone to refute the picture of the disengaged subject (1989, p. 514). The deconstructions of Derrida, the importance of the other and relationship (albeit in different ways) in the work of Bakhtin and Levinas, to Heidegger's delineation of the immersion of beings in Being, and to Richard Rorty, writing of the contingency of selfhood, all point to an impermanent, contingent and constructed subject whose identity is constituted and changed continually in relationship rather than a unified and separate subject. From selfhood the emphasis has shifted to alterity, from unity and identity to difference.

We can perhaps begin to see our selves as fictions. As the neuropsychologist Paul Broks says:

> From a neuroscience perspective we are all divided and discontinuous. The mental processes underlying our sense of self—feelings, thoughts, memories—are scattered through different zones of the brain. There is no special point of convergence. No cockpit of the soul. No soul-pilot. They come together as a work of fiction. A human being is a story-telling machine. The self is a story. [2003, p. 41]

The idea of self as fiction is found in many places. Daniel Dennet describes self as the "centre of narrative gravity"; the neurologist Michael Gazzaniga writes of the "interpreter function" within the left hemisphere of the brain. It takes a writer of fiction, however, to suggest: "it may be that to understand ourselves as fictions is to understand ourselves as fully as we can" (Winterson, 1995, p. 60).

Jerome Bruner, the godfather of cognitive psychology, has written widely about the narrative creation of the self, which brings together many of the features of self-creation, both in development and in repair, that we have discussed. He believes that it is "through narrative that we create and re-create selfhood, that self is a product of our telling and not some essence to be delved for in the recesses of subjectivity" (2002, p. 86). He describes how self-making is both from the inside and from the outside. Memory, feelings, ideas, beliefs and subjectivity from the inside come together with the responses and expectations of others and culture from the outside. Our selves are then constantly constructed and reconstructed to meet the necessities of the situations we encounter, such re-creations being modelled by our past memories and our expectations of the future. Within this understanding of the interdependence of self and world he also includes intersubjectivity, saying: "it hardly requires a postmodern leap to conclude, accordingly, that self is also other" (ibid., p. 66). In support of this idea of the relational self, he cites cases where sufferers from diseases that impair the sense of self appear to lose not only their own sense of self but also a sense of other (ibid., p. 86; see also Sacks, 1973). Again, it is a creative writer who brings together all the important aspects of storytelling. Ursula Le Guin tells us: "All of us have to invent our lives, make them up, imagine them. We need to be taught those skills. We need guides to show us how. If we don't, our lives get made up for us by other people" (2004, p. 208). Just as we need our parents to teach us emotional regulation, so we need the encouragement of story to foster imagination and the narrative aspect of our selves. And Le Guin points out that this applies both to our individual selves and to cultures which are defined through story, the myths that are then used to teach the people how to be members of that culture.

Conclusion

A recent article in a journal dedicated to "Models of Self", somewhat tongue in cheek, refers to "the cognitive self, the conceptual self, the contextualised self, the core self, the dialogic self, the ecological self, the embodied self, the emergent self, the empirical self, the existential self, the extended self, the fictional self, the full-grown self, the interpersonal self, the material self, the narrative self, the philosophical self, the private self, the representational self, the rock bottom essential self, the semiotic self, the social self, the transparent self and the verbal self" (Strawson, 1999). And this makes no mention of the synaptic self of Joseph Le Doux, who suggests that the self is the reflection of patterns of interconnectivity between neurons in the brain. Perhaps the only shared characteristic of all these descriptions is that they are all constructions. Thus the views of self in contemporary Western discourse in philosophy and science do not seem inimical to that of Buddhism. If the sense of self is upheld according to the Buddhist view by craving, conceit and false views, perhaps Western approaches may be said to have come to terms intellectually with views of self rather better than they have emotionally with craving and conceit. Contemporary views of self are, as we have seen, most definitely no longer those of a single, unitary and permanent self, and everywhere we find a distinction between transactional self and self-image or self-concept. Yet our conceit of "I" and our craving of "mine" would not appear to have caught up yet with our intellectual knowledge. Does this matter? I think it does, both on the philosophical and on the personal level. For though views may have changed, our daily lives have not, and if our changing views are not accompanied by attention to the emotional reinforcements of I and mine, to the old suffering will be added new suffering of uncertainty and resistance to the new views. As self is separated from world and other, so it appropriates and attempts to dominate both world and other. Similar separations are mirrored even in the interior individual world, with the domination of head or intellect over body and feeling, until we are alienated not only from our environment externally but also from our embodied existence and our own experience. We become afraid of living.

Paradoxically, along with the weakening of the certainty of world and of the punctual self, the West has seen both a rise in nihilistic thought and a reactionary emotional clinging to the concept of self. Despite the increasing theoretical dispersal of self over a wide area, intrapersonal, interpersonal and even transpersonal, we also see an increased emphasis upon the self, on actualisation of its potential. In practice, the self as construct or even as process has itself been defensively reified and reconsolidated. The generation of humanistic psychology has been termed narcissistic in the most pejorative sense, that of the "me" generation. Although the sense of self is no longer unitary, yet the operational view of it as an egocentric centre of operations has been strengthened: theoretical models of the widely-distributed self seem to be accompanied by an ever stronger practical and emotional focus on the interiority and individuality of that self. Yet this does not seem to increase happiness or well-being. Psychotherapists deal daily with issues of depression, loss of meaning, lack of self-esteem, and narcissism.

Narcissism and egotism are a defence against inadequacy or loss. In Buddhist terms such defence is unnecessary since the loss is illusory, a loss of something which never existed in the first place, for the self itself is not an existent reality but merely a mental construction which falsely experiences itself as separate and then feels its own perceived groundlessness as a lack. For Buddhism, investigation of the mental constructions which give rise to this constructed sense of self reveals its emptiness; thus at one stroke it loosens both the conceptual proliferation which supports the sense of self, that self itself, and the anxiety unconsciously defending its fragility. What is left is not nothing but a greater non-egocentric grounding, as one writer, David Loy beautifully describes: "If each link of pratitya-samutpada is conditioned by all the others, then to become completely groundless is also to become completely grounded, not in some particular but in the whole network of interdependent relations that constitute the world. The supreme irony of my struggle to ground myself is that it cannot succeed because I am already grounded in the totality" (Loy, 1998, p. 209).

Buddhism has in its long history not only effected the intellectual deconstruction of substantial views of world, self and their relationship but has also instituted methods of practice for vitiating the emotional attachment to such views. It engages both with the philosophical and psychological sense of lack and its concurrent desire, for the philosophical and the psychological are inextricably interwoven. We see how belief in self is upheld by desire to be and to have a self, and how from the central pivot of identification with a self the notion of mine and the entire egocentric world arises.

For the Western view the perceived loss of self may well lead either to nihilism or to a reactive narcissistic grasping of self;[9] whereas the realisation that self and world are interdependent and ultimately empty allows one not merely to ride on the processual wave but to be it. When world is not viewed from an egocentric position, self may be seen not as a solitary unit but as immanent and embedded within a larger network of relationship with world, and both self and even death take on a different aspect. For, as the anthropologist Gregory Bateson pointed out in an unusual Western exposition of interdependence: "the individual nexus of pathways which I call 'me' is no longer so precious because that nexus is only part of a larger mind" (1972, p. 440). The bridge between self and emptiness, which carries one over the abyss of nihilism, is interconnection and interdependence. In a different but very Buddhist-sounding description of this, the neurologist Paul Broks writes: "Minds emerge from process and interaction, not substance. In a sense we inhabit the spaces between things. We subsist in emptiness. A beautiful liberating thought, nothing to be afraid of" (2003, p. 50).

This may lead to a middle way between subjectivity and objectivity, one that escapes the extremism of either side, a non-dual view, which may evade the Western dilemma of embracing either an extreme objectivism or an equally extreme subjectivism.[10] This returns us yet again to the beautiful and succinct lines of the Japanese Buddhist Dogen in the thirteenth century, expressing both the impoverishment of the egocentric view and an alternative to it, a description of both the self to be abandoned and the enlightened self:

To practise and confirm all things by conveying one's self to them is illusion; for all things to advance forward and practise and confirm the self is enlightenment... To learn the Buddha Way is to learn one's own self. To learn one's self is to forget one's self. To forget one's self is to be confirmed by all dharmas. [*Genjokoan*, Abe & Waddell, 2002, p. 133]

We are encouraged in Buddhist mindfulness and meditation to discover these processes through regaining moment-to-moment contact with our experience, with the flow of experience rather than with the conceptuality with which we commonly cloak it. With the intention of non-egocentrism, mindfulness and meditation encourage our awareness to participate fully in present experience. To us in the West today, ever more separated from our experience by conceptuality, expectation and alienation, this is an important message. In our often desperate search for meaning, we have sometimes lost the experience itself. At every turn we are bombarded by encouragement to cut off from our current experience, to plaster over our surroundings with other images, to drown out the sound of wind and birds with the noises emitted by the earphones clamped over our ears. We need to relearn how to pay attention. If we can let go of our self-image, we may regain our experience. With no need to defend illusory selves, we may open to other, and reconnecting with our experience, discover there is no lack. The question of self is a question of being, not of having.

Notes

1. In a most interesting recent collection of essays on this topic, P. Young-Eisendrath & J. A. Hall (eds.), *The Book of the Self: Person, Pretext & Process*, one contribution alone is dedicated to the terminology of Ego and Self, and that merely amongst Freudians and Jungians. For helpful suggestions in agreed terminology, see Galin (2003).
2. From John Locke, *Essay Concerning Human Understanding*, II.27.9.
3. Tibetan Buddhism is divided into different schools, each with distinctive practices and teachings. The dGe Lugs approach, probably the best known in the West due to its head, the Dalai Lama, tends to be the most scholastic.
4. See Chapter Three; also Varela (1999). The research he refers to is that by M. J. Meany et al. (1996).

5. J. Austin, author of *Zen and the Brain*, quoted in Horgan, 2003, p.130.
6. Notably Sue Hamilton (1996) and Mervyn Sprung (1979).
7. Traleg Rinpoche in a talk presented at a conference on Buddhism and Psychotherapy at Maitripa Centre, Melbourne, Australia, November 2003.
8. Such as those from Systems Theory, from the neuroscientific work of Gerald Edelman (1992) and from Margaret Donaldson's psychological description (1992).
9. "The deep problem... with the merely theoretical discovery of mind without self in as powerful and technical a context as late twentieth century science is that it is almost impossible to avoid embracing some form of nihilism." (Varela, Thompson & Rosch, 1991, p. 127.
10. Heidegger describes this in "The Age of the World Picture", whereby in this age of great subjectivism and individualism, there is at the same time great objectivism, as the world has become impoverished as "representation". See Heidegger, 1977, p. 128.

PART III
ACTION

Introduction

Living is my job and my art.

(Montaigne, *Essais II*, Chapter VI)

The end of man is an action and not a thought...

(Carlyle, *Sartor Resartus II*, Chapter VI)

So far we have contemplated new views coming from contemporary science concerning the way our minds work, so that, in accord with this new understanding, we may re-vision and re-form our relationship with our bodies, our emotions and our environment, physical, social and cultural. We see that our selves are ongoing process, built up of embodiment, emotions and thought, and reliant upon environment, society and intersubjectivity. We see that selves, both the feeling of self and the self image we build onto this, come into being mostly non-consciously and dependent upon experience, and that, most importantly, they are plastic and transformable to some degree. In dialogue with this new knowledge, I have also turned to ancient Buddhist ideas and practices which are, in some areas, impressively resonant with this. They endorse both the possibility and the necessity of emotional and attentional education in support of happiness and wellbeing, and demonstrate that many of our current goals in education fall short of meeting the needs of our embodiment and our emotionality, failing to see at one pole how we are very much part of nature rather than outside it, and at the other pole the special opportunities provided by our humanity. Evolution is now carried by culture as well as nature. Evolved consciousness brings us the possibility of changing ourselves. The findings of science should encourage us to pay attention to both these poles — animality, belonging and a certain humility, and the potential of awareness and self creation.

In these final chapters I want to reflect on future action, less on *what* than on *how*. If we are to use this new knowledge and the long-standing Buddhist practices of awareness and attention skilfully in the service of wellbeing, I suggest that the major changes may be not so much what we do as how we do it. So I would like to weave some new voices into the song: the articulation of attention, awareness and the feminine voice, and of creativity and imagination. Both the mind sciences and Buddhist practices show that human nature and self-consciousness allow us some space for self-creation. This is the action called for, but in order for this to be a step forward towards greater wellbeing rather than a deluded ego trip towards increasing alienation, we need to pay attention to the way to advance. We need to learn to pay careful consideration to our embodiment, to our emotions, and to our relationships with one another, with the world we live in, and with our ideas and culture, so that we may use all the space we have for wise choice rather than unthinking reaction. Above all we need imagination and creativity. Without imagination there can be neither empathy nor the ability to see things as other than they appear at any given moment. We need imagination and empathy to envision transformation.

CHAPTER NINE

Attention, receptivity and the feminine voice

Remain sitting at your table and listen. Do not even listen; simply wait. Do not even wait; be quite still and solitary. The world will freely offer itself to you to be unmasked; it has no choice; it will roll in ecstasy at your feet.

(Franz Kafka, quoted in Baker, 2004, p. 293)

First, a principle of attention, simply that. A faith that if we look and look we will be surprised and we will be rewarded.

(Franz Kafka, quoted in Baker, 2004, p. 48)

… A man becomes his attentions. His observations and curiosity, they make and remake him.

Etymology: Curious, related to cure, once meant "carefully observant". Maybe a tonic of curiosity would counter my numbing sense that life inevitably creeps towards the absurd. Absurd, by the way, derives from a Latin word meaning "deaf, dulled". Maybe the road could provide a therapy through observation of the ordinary and obvious, a means whereby the outer eye opens an inner one. STOP, LOOK, LISTEN, the old railroad signs warned. Whitman calls it "the profound lesson of reception".

(Heat Moon, 1982, p. 17)

The death of the self of which the great writers speak is no violent act. It is merely the slow cessation of the will's spirits and the intellect's chatter: it is waiting like a hollow bell with stilled tongue. *Fuge, tace. Quiesce.* The waiting itself is the thing.

(Dillard, 1974, p. 226)

L et us, for a moment, pay attention to attention. It is with close attention to our embodiment and our enworldedness that we notice the bias of our emotions and the construction of our selves; it is through gaining awareness of our automatic actions and the projections we have repressed that we can become less determined by them; it is through the cultivation and education of attention that we may transform our emotions and our selves. Buddhist teachings have long proposed education in attention, and psychotherapy offers emotional tutorial through paying attention to what is overlooked, ignored or actively denied. Neuroscience now tells us that paying attention can become embodied — those networks of neural firing most frequently used become those most easily activated; links that are frequently made will commonly activate together, most significantly when activated in conjunction with the activation of attentional mechanisms. So the transformations sought through the teachings and practices of Buddhism are seen to be actually instantiated. Thich Nhat Hanh has warned against too much cathartic expression of unhealthy emotions such as anger within some psychotherapies, suggesting that it will water the seeds of future anger. It would appear that he is right, not only metaphorically but also literally, on the neurological level.

Considering *processes* of awareness and attention, rather than the content of objects of attention, is uncommon in our culture. It leads away from the well-trodden paths that focus on information and activity and ends rather than means. Western culture has a very strong tendency to "fill" time; time left to itself is considered time wasted. From early in childhood we are encouraged to do and to have. Even in recreation and relaxation we seek activity, and if not active, then passive entertainment such as television, video and electronic games. We are rarely encouraged just to stop and be, notice what is around, take in our surroundings, and let our intuition and our imagination guide us. Let us listen to William James once more:

> The faculty of voluntarily bringing back a wandering attention over and over again is the very root of judgement, character and will. No one is *compos sui* if he have it not. An education which should improve this faculty would be the education par excellence. [1890/1981, p. 401]

Our standard education is sadly far from such excellence.[1] If attention to attention itself, to awareness and to emotion is to become restored in our culture, these practices must be considered early. The importance of emotional regulation has huge implications for child-rearing practices and for early education. While it also has important implications for psychotherapy (how to repair dysfunction in early development), how much better it would be if we could eliminate the need for repair. New understanding of the processes of development, the importance of EQ as well as IQ, and the significance of attention needs to be fed back into education and social services in the form of help for parents, play for children, and an education based on how we learn, not just on what we need to know. There are some hopeful signs.

In 1995 Daniel Goleman published a book called *Emotional Intelligence*. In this work he summarised the research that was showing the importance of emotion for development and for cognition. The timely popularity of the book brought the concept into language and consideration. Emotional intelligence, he said, refers to the way we handle our emotions and relationships, and he designated four parts to it: self awareness (or knowing what we are feeling), managing those feelings, empathy (or knowing how we are impacting upon other people), and handling relationships. While this seems quite obvious, the idea that it is necessary to teach it is not. However, since that time, projects which have taken account of emotional literacy and fostered social-emotional learning within the school curriculum have been found to be helpful, not only for their psychological and social outcomes but also in enhancing the scholastic achievement of the pupils. Just as Buddhists see destructive emotions as those which cloud the mind, so Goleman describes how emotions are more powerful than thoughts in "capturing" the attention, taking space within the narrow band of attention away from objects of learning. He demonstrates that there is a direct connection between a child's social-emotional learning and his or her academic progress. Today there are literally thousands of such projects in schools throughout the world. However, this is by no means standard.[2] Such programmes take account of social-emotional factors while teaching academic subjects, repeating the lessons over the entire period of a child's school years, changing the content in a developmentally appropriate manner. Other programmes introduce silence and mindfulness into elementary schools as an aid to acknowledging feelings.

Reading Allan Schore's important work on attachment and development, which brings together neurological, biological and psychological research, one cannot but notice the import he places on the right hemisphere of the brain. The research he quotes reveals the preeminent role of the right hemisphere on the control of both sympathetic and parasympathetic aspects of the autonomic nervous system, and in the development of emotional intelligence, empathy, autobiographical memory and self-reflection. As we have seen, he writes of non-conscious right brain to right brain communications between parent and infant, which develop regulation (or in poor cases dysregulation) of autonomic function. He demonstrates the importance of emotional regulation and development for actual healthy physiological growth, and with its influential impact on the healthy development of the immune system, for the future physical and mental health of the organism. He has indeed suggested that the emotion-processing right brain should be seen as the neurobiological substrate of Freud's dynamic unconscious (2003b, vol. 2). He endorses a view of this as a relational unconscious, evolving out of a constantly changing but ever-present process of somatic, affective and cognitive experience in interactive dialogue with internal and external objects, and suggests that we should speak not of *the* unconscious but of multiple levels of conscious and unconscious in continual interactive process. Whereas the left hemisphere, dealing predominantly with sequential linear processing and linguistic information, has commonly been considered the essence of the human mind, Schore suggests that neuroscience should follow Freud's injunction to look beneath words and give more consideration to the right brain. He advocates that Freud's dictum of the centrality of unconscious processes in everyday life should be interpreted to mean that the right brain is dominant in humans, and that the most fundamental problems of human existence cannot be understood without addressing this primordial realm.

Reading this reminds me that the right hemisphere of the brain has often been considered the "feminine" side of the brain. The disregard of this side runs alongside the lack of respect given to other qualities seen as "feminine". While I am loath to enter the sinking sands of gender politics, feminist polemic, political correctness and patriarchal backlash, I truly believe that there is an imbalance here that needs to be corrected if we are to flourish and find wellbeing. This involves, I believe, something which, for want of a better term and in understanding of all its dangerous implications, I have come to call the feminine voice.

What is the feminine voice? I believe that there are qualities which we may in conventional understanding and speech correctly term "feminine" in contradistinction to those termed "masculine". I think that our reception of many of these "feminine" qualities, indeed our labelling of them, is not essential but has arisen from convention, society and expectation. Most importantly, I believe they are not the exclusive property of women but belong to us all. Perhaps one can envision a sliding spectrum of qualities, masculine one pole, feminine the other, and each of us, man or woman, is placed (or place ourselves) somewhere on this scale. That these qualities are largely artificially human-designated does not matter; that their labels are usually man-made and rarely woman-made may. For they are the exclusive property neither of men nor of women but belong to both and, I contend, need to be equally valued. That the so-called feminine values have been undervalued is the problem, not that they are designated as feminine. That such values have been used to define and to limit what is considered "womanly" or "manly" is the problem, not their designation. This has wounded women obviously, and men less obviously but still profoundly. In a patriarchal world we have had a hierarchy of values, through the greater valorisation of one term—the masculine—at the expense of the other—the feminine. What we all need and must surely seek now is a plurality of values, a revalorization of the feminine, and a turn to ways of connection and co-operation rather than competition.

In the battles against patriarchy, feminism has achieved so much for which women can be grateful. My daughter undoubtedly lives in a world of less restriction, social and legal, and greater possibility than the one I entered at adulthood. Many battles have been won. Yet there is a paradox. That I use the metaphor of war exposes the extent of the problem: that our very language, which Heidegger called our house of being, is thoroughly saturated with masculine bias. The depth of this problem is the source of the paradox. Ironically, such gains for women have at times been won only through a loss of the feminine voice, through winning by taking on the qualities of the opposed masculine. To become heard, the voice has had to become masculine, sometimes strident, often combative, taking on those very patriarchal qualities which previously silenced its own. Just recently I attended an academic conference on postmodern poetry. I expected that both poetry and the postmodern would and should embrace plurality and the feminine voice, but I watched as few women among many men, in dark suits, read dense intellectual papers quickly, with great intelligence but little warmth, with no sense of embodiment or passion. Reason rules, or attempts to rule our lives, with the inevitable periodic eruptions of repressed unreason as the ignored shadow bursts forth. Our emotions, our sense of embodiment, our intuition of our place in the environment, all have been more or less ignored and placed in thrall to our reason and our self-image. Everything becomes their possession, either their potential or their terror. From the centre of self-image and possessed knowledge the world is imagined. Alienated from participation, walled in the separated and separative self, the world is out there as adversary or theatre set. As we have seen above, it is not only Buddhist thought which tells us that this alienation is illusory; current Western science is telling us that reality and our perception of it are very different from what we thought.

So what are these "feminine" qualities that belong to us all? I would say that they are best described by the Yin qualities of the Chinese Taoist philosophy, the necessary counterbalance to Yang: receptivity as opposed to activity, listening as opposed to discourse, being in contrast to doing, collaboration rather than competition, connection and integration rather than analysis, and a greater attention to feeling and intuition rather than dependence only on cognition and reason. As one enumerates these qualities, it is easy to see

how devalued they have become, and how feminists, acknowledging them as devalued, have understandably resisted identification
with them. As Fritjof Capra wrote in 1976:

> Our culture has consistently favoured *yang*, or masculine, values over
> *yin*, or feminine, counterparts. We have favoured self assertion over
> integration, analysis over synthesis, rational knowledge over intui-
> tive wisdom, science over religion, competition over cooperation,
> expansion over conservation, and so on. This one-sided development
> has now reached a highly alarming stage, a crisis of social, ecological,
> moral and spiritual dimensions. [p. xvi]

Listening and reflection have been considered passive, squeezed
out in the emphasis on discourse, on being heard. Contemporary
life encourages us to be too concerned with what we have to say
to take the time to listen and reflect—on ourselves, our bodies, our
feelings for each other and for the non-human world. Similarly, we
are too busy doing to look around, to reflect, feel, and receive. To
repeat yet again the words Dogen said some seven hundred years
ago:

> To practice and confirm all things by conveying one's self to them is
> illusion; for all things to advance forward and practise and confirm
> the self is enlightenment.

We are so concerned with the illusion, with impressing ourselves, our
views and our actions onto the ten thousand things that we cannot
allow them to touch us, allow ourselves to be enlightened.

As we saw with selves, it is a question of being, not of having or
doing. D. W. Winnicott, one of the most perceptive psychoanalysts,
stated: "The male element *does* while the female element (in males
and females) *is*" (1971, p. 81). Mark Epstein, in his recent book *Open
to Desire*, describes beautifully how desire in its longing for comple-
tion is ultimately in search of being. We can never grasp our subjectivity. If we try to grasp or own our experience, we turn it into an
object and lose it, stripping it of its subjective quality. "The only way
to know it is to be it" (2005, p. 173).

It is instructive that in their book *Mindfulness-Based Cognitive
Therapy for Depression*, Segal, Williams and Teasdale state that the
task of mindfulness training is teaching individuals to become more
aware of their modes of mind, and to instil the skills to move from

an unhelpful mode to one more conducive to liberation from depression and its origins. They speak of the two main modes of mind: those of "doing" and of "being" (2002, pp. 69–75). Doing modes, which they also call "driven" modes, are triggered when the mind sees a mismatch between actual and desired states of affairs; when the mind dwells on discrepancies between an idea of how things are and how they are wished to be or "ought" to be. In doing mode the mind is driven to reduce the perceived gap between how things are and how we would wish them to be. In contrast, in being mode the quality is accepting and allowing of what is, similar to what some Buddhist teachings call "one taste", the equanimous acceptance, neither grasping nor aversive, of whatever arises. The relation of this to the feminine voice, I hope, is obvious.

We need to receive and include this feminine voice. Not, as so often happens, in a rush to endorse emotionality and intuition at the expense of reason, a mere exchange of one pole of imbalance for another, but in a search for balance between the two hemispheres of the brain, between being and doing, and between the masculine and feminine voices. This could support the kind of attention of non-judgemental awareness and receptive openness we find in meditation and mindfulness. In practice, meditation, with its exercises of deep listening and receptive mindfulness, embodies such theory. Indeed, mindfulness and meditation support a different way of knowing. Rather than sustaining a totality of knowledge, they are concerned with a quality of attention; rather than supporting singleness of concentration, they are concerned with an equable and widespread attention to whatever arises.[3] As mentioned before, it was this kind of attention that Freud called for in psychoanalysis, an "evenly hovering attention" which is receptive to free association, to embodiment, to the non-conscious. Both Buddhism and psychotherapy encourage listening; they allow us an unusual opportunity to listen and be listened to, deeply and non-judgementally. Before springing to action or engaging with cognitive judgement, we can allow ourselves to "feel" the experience. Strangely, this may not only alter the judgements and actions we finally take, but may transform and enhance the whole experience. In Buddhist meditation, we listen to ourselves, to the way our minds work; in psychotherapy, we listen in company with an other or others more to the *contents* of our minds, the scripts and beliefs that constrain us and the emotions we have ignored, even to our unheard bodies. Maybe such open attention and receptivity can lead us to a practice close to the body but embedded in the world, of permeable boundary touching and being touched, reaching for the stars yet rooted in earth, a practice of earth and sky, of heart open to play and being played upon in body, speech and mind, a practice of active passivity, the opening to the world of which Dogen speaks.

Such a receptive stance may help us in other ways in the search for happiness. Paradoxically, a little silence and solitude may help to heal contemporary alienation. As a recent writer noted of solitude: "No amount of group therapy, study of interpersonal relationships, self-improvement exercises, personal training in the gym, can assuage the loneliness of those who cannot bear to be alone" (Colegate, 2002, p. xv). Similarly, another writer speaking of the way to heal in the aftermath of 9/11 says: "The way in—and out—lay in silence. The rare, unmarketable gift of silence. For the duration of four hours, four minutes, four blessed heartbeats" (Sojourner, 2002, p. 165).

This attention and receptivity is a kind of humility, a listening that is willing to learn—from nature and from others—rather than imposing upon them. It is the participatory voice found in deep ecology and in Biomimicry, a path for science that learns from nature and is constrained by sustainability and understanding of ecology. The steps that Biomimicry endorses are those of Quieting, immersing ourselves in nature, Listening, then Echoing and Stewardship. But the first and most important steps are those of Quieting and Listening (Benyus, 1997). This way is a way of opening up, of ceasing to be a spectator and knowing oneself to be an actor implicated in the play of world and other.

It is this kind of listening and non-judgemental acceptance that forms the crucible for healing in psychotherapy. Before there can be any transformation, we need the steps of careful listening to uncover the hidden, followed by acknowledgement and articulation. Only then can we move forward to integration and change. This takes courage. The inner may appear more frightening than the outer—especially in a culture of evasion, of filling every quiet minute. But we will never find happiness unless we can listen to unhappiness. The way out is the way through, and each step alters the path.

Such a listening would provide a strong antidote to the technological thinking at the foundation of recent history and thought. For it is a commitment to attention, to receptivity as response. In contrast to a voice that is masterly, hierarchical and logical, concerned with identity, separation and independence, the feminine voice is more aware of and concerned with difference and interdependence, response and relationship, community and complementarity. To bring these two voices, statement and response, speaking and listening, into dialogue and to give equal valuation to each would be to enrich dialogue and daily living. We need to seek steadiness and stability, a centre from which to respond best to the changing world. This requires *practice*; the cultivation that we saw was the root of meditation. Mindfulness is a practice whereby we can change ourselves both physiologically and psychologically, something that current research programmes are confirming (see Appendix 2). Most of the practices now being endorsed in the search for happiness involve a re-orientation of attention. This has beneficial effects both on chemical processes in the lowering of levels of stress hormones such as cortisol, and also in the resetting of neuronal networks. Practices such as formal meditation itself, mindfulness-derived practices such as those of Jon Kabat Zinn and of Mindfulness Based Cognitive Behavioural Therapy, and Heart Math are all, at root, practices of attention and awareness. Paying attention to attention itself, they retune the way we think and react by turning the emphasis upon the process itself rather than on its content.

I believe that in the West we lack the traditions of cultivation as practice. Religion and philosophy have been about belief and ritual, and the rituals have increasingly become public, with ever less to do with quiet individual daily practice. Indeed, I think that the Western espousal of meditation and mindfulness practices has often displayed a tendency towards mystification, seeking in meditation moments of transcendence, with inevitable disappointment as the practice turns out to be quieter, less dramatic, more everyday—but no less valuable. It may be helpful to turn to the East, to such practices as the many ways or *do* of Japanese traditions: the way of flower arranging, the way of tea, of calligraphy and of the many martial arts. All aspects of daily life may become a "way" of self-cultivation; the distinction lies in intention, attention and practice.

Notes

1. In a hopeful project contradicting this, and one which is covertly, if not overtly, influenced by a knowledge of Buddhist ideas and practice, Professor Guy Claxton has recently published a booklet entitled *Building Learning Power*, and under the same title instigated a programme in several schools offering a new and creative approach to learning to learn. It is based on the 4 Rs of learning power: Resilience, Resourcefulness, Reflectiveness and Reciprocity. Resilience, which is founded on awareness and attention, has key points of contemplating, stilling, questioning values and managing distraction. Resourcefulness encourages questioning, linking, imagining and reasoning, suggesting key points of curiosity, adventure and play. Reflectiveness supports planning, revision and awareness of the process of learning itself and the self as learner. Reciprocity stresses interdependence, collaboration, empathy and listening. See Guy Claxton, *Building Learning Power* (Bristol: TLO, 2002; available from TLO Ltd., Henleaze House, Hanbury Road, Bristol BS9 4PN).

2. See Goleman (1995). Further information about projects may be obtained from CASEL (Collaborative for Academic, Social and Emotional Learning) and from The George Lucas Educational Foundation.

3. The advantages of such a different way of knowing and organising are explored and celebrated particularly in the writings of Mary Catherine Bateson, such as *Composing a Life* and *Peripheral Vision*.

CHAPTER TEN

Inconclusion:
creativity, imagination and metaphor

Creativity has much to do with experience, observation and imagination, and if any one of those key elements is missing, it doesn't work.

(Dylan, 2004, p. 121)

We can begin to live differently. We can give birth to deep change, creating a commitment of compassion towards all living things. Our human-centred point of view can evolve into an Earth-centred one. Is this too much to dream? Who imposes restraint on our imagination?

(Williams, 2001, p. 162)

...because happiness is not an ideal of reason but of imagination.

(Kant, 1949)

B reakdown of understanding demands us, if we are brave enough, to respond authentically to the challenge. It asks us to let go of creaking certainties which no longer support us and to follow questioning into unknowing, trusting the support of our experience of embodiment, emotion and environment. Forced to examine our previously unacknowledged preconceptions, we may be led into a wider perspective. It is a task of constant and consistent questioning. In science and in consciousness studies the results of research fit uneasily within our previously accepted horizons.[1] New wine seeks new bottles, and attempts to squeeze the new into the accustomed confines of the comfortably familiar do not lead to wellbeing.

If, as Whitehead suggested, all of Western philosophy is a series of footnotes to Plato, then we are now seeing a serious convergence of efforts by philosophers—both European post-Nietzschean thinkers and American pragmatists—and scientists to construct new paths and new texts. Many of the most interesting minds of the last century have signposted this: Heidegger wrote of the end of metaphysics, seeking the close of what he termed the ontotheological tradition; Derrida pointed towards the ending of what he termed metaphysics of presence. The Cartesian separation of mind and body, substance and extension, and Newtonian mechanics belong to an earlier paradigm. Now we need a new intellectual framework which can bring together first person subjective and third person objective understandings in a pattern which can close the gap between theory and practice, science and philosophy, and embodied experience and intellect. If attention may give a foundation, perhaps creativity and imagination may afford the springboard for extension and development towards what we may be, as well as an understanding of what and where we are now.

All this change is not new, only new—or news—to us. That things were ever so is shown by the similarity of Buddha's teachings two millennia ago. Yet if all that persists is change, can we not acknowledge it, live with it? The world has always been, is now, and may well remain replete with mystery and areas beyond the reach of any contemporary explanation. Rather than trying to tame our world, can we learn to live within it? There is so much that is larger than our selves, that we do not know, but we persist in trying to live as if we did.

Indeed, whilst I have stated the often repeated fact about consciousness studies, that most of its scientists are physicalists, at
present we still lack a proper theory of the nature of the physical
world. So many of the basic questions that we consistently ignore,
think we understand and take for granted actually remain unan-
swered. What is physicality? What is consciousness? What is life?
Since the overthrow of classical Newtonian physics by relativity
theory and quantum mechanics, "we have every reason to believe
that our best current physical theory is wrong not merely in its minor
details but in major respects", according to leading thinkers (Hanna
& Thompson, 2003). The claim that the mental is reducible to the
physical is widely accepted, yet in the absence of a true theory of the
nature of the physical such a claim is indefensible. Noam Chomsky
noted this, saying that materialism can only be a coherent position
if its adherents can tell us what counts as physical or material. He
extends this critique to a more general conclusion that "in the absence
of a coherent notion of 'body', the traditional mind-body problem has
no conceptual status" (2000, p. 85; quoted in Hanna & Thompson).
And this only concerns our human lives. When we travel further out,
the language of cosmology is the language of poetry to laymen—
curvature of space-time, black holes, dark energy, dark matter. Yet
we mostly respond to such challenges to accepted ways of thought in
Freudian terms, with repression in the defensive form of denial. We
attempt to live as if we were in control both of our lives and identities
and our world. As reality is not like that, we suffer. Even when we
are happy, happiness passes and it seems as if there is always something more just out of reach.

Here we need attention and creativity: to acknowledge what we
do not understand and cannot control, and thus to liberate ourselves
to embrace mystery. Let God stand for all that is beyond our understanding and domination rather than as a father figure who will keep
us safe. We can continue to reject and repress what is larger than us,
what we don't understand, or with humility and imagination we can
receive it. As Santideva suggested in the eighth century, why can we
not consider ourselves as the limbs of life?

As noted in Chapter One, in a project much influenced by contemporary anti-essentialist philosophies, the radical Christian theologian Don Cupitt suggested that religion should be viewed not as
truth but as a guide for living, describing it as a set of spiritual tools

for enhancing our lives in a way similar to that of art, and calling it "an experiment in selfhood".[2] There have been many other similar suggestions. The Buddhist writer Stephen Batchelor has asked whether in the transformation of Buddhism into a form responsive to the plurality and individualism of the contemporary anguish, we can envisage a democracy of the imagination in which each individual ceases to be a passive recipient of spiritual truths and becomes instead their active creator. Later in the same article, he echoes such thoughts even more closely, stating: "Practice is a process of self creation."[3] Both suggest that today we are being asked to become the creators of our own religious lives. However, we are not isolated creators; such creation must take place within community.

Again this finds echoes in the Dalai Lama's writings concerning what he calls *basic spirituality*, the cultivation of those fundamental qualities of goodness, kindness, compassion and caring that he terms *genuine Dharma*. He states that engaging in any method of training to bring about such inner discipline within one's mind is the essence of a religious life, and that leading a spiritual life depends on whether or not one is successful in bringing about a disciplined state of mind which may be translated into one's daily actions. Indeed, the seeds of this are clearly stated, as we have noticed, in the opening words of one of the most popular and most translated Pali texts, the *Dhammapada*:

We are what we think.
All that we are arises with our thoughts.
With our thoughts we make the world.

We can never control the external world; indeed, to acknowledge and accept that fact is one of the foundations of the first ennobling truth, to truly know that life in *samsara* is unsatisfactory and causes suffering. However we can work with our minds to change our relationship with the world.

It would seem that genuine Dharma or basic spirituality may help us here to embody a different approach, one of relationship and complementarity which might provide a middle path between many physical and metaphysical dualities such as appearance and reality, eternalism and nihilism, subject and object, mind and body, asceticism and sensuality. It may help us evade what Daniel Dennet has called "the absolutism that sees only two possibilities" (2003, p. 271).

This may help us avoid the pendulum swing between either-or and all or nothing. It can support us to swim in process as a middle way between the hazards of Scylla and Charybdis, extreme positions such as fundamentalism versus relativism. It may offer us a different understanding and a different set of models. It may provide practices of attention that can help us to understand our own models, beliefs and identifications which are often so deeply embedded and identified with that we are no longer aware of them. Such deep attention may reveal their constructed nature, thus loosening our identification with them, leaving us space for choice, change and creation. Such changes in practices and understanding may help us to embrace a different stance towards embodiment, emotion and environment, one that may enable us to live differently, more happily, with attention, humility and participation. Wittgenstein sought a philosophy that would show the fly the way of escape from the fly bottle, a philosophy that could be laid down when its task was achieved. Such an image is a complement to the Buddhist metaphor of the teaching as a raft to be left behind when the river is crossed.

An experiment in selfhood will be very different in the context of the twenty-first century in the West from that of Asia at a far earlier time, and an experiment which is out of synch with its own time and context will not be a useful experiment. Cultural psychology, in the words of Ciaran Benson, presents what you are as a function of where you are (2001). Like Batchelor and Cupitt, Benson too suggests that the ideal psychological life from a contemporary cultural psychological perspective is one with the character of an artistic project "where the meaning of a life is no more summarisable in words than a symphony or a painting, but which is nonetheless discernible to connoisseurs of living" (*ibid.*, p. 100). A "contemporary experiment in selfhood" will take note of the feminine voice, for it will be one that is not just (in that ugly late twentieth century term) "proactive", but one which is in the very best sense receptive. A receptivity which is openness to what is other: not self, not known, whether this is external other beings or land, or internal, unconscious. For to be truly creative is to open ourselves up to the unknown. In life as in a work of art, creativity embodies a double journey, a passage from the known to the unknown and a return from the formless, the as yet unknown and ineffable, back to communicable form. An imaginative extension of the known into the not yet known involves a re-description of the familiar.

In this way of living which Cupitt calls "cosmic democracy" and Batchelor "democracy of the imagination", everything is open to attention, to mental questioning and that careful observation which is one of the etymological roots of the word "religion". We have to create our lives today, not copy a given script. We may, and perhaps must, bring receptive questioning attention to language. We need to examine all the old dead metaphors which we no longer see as symbols, with which we identify. We need to revivify old metaphors and embrace new ones, engaging with them from the foundation of our aware embodiment and with our emotion. Above all, we need to enjoy them imaginatively and to know them again as symbols. We need new metaphors to truly "carry us across". But more importantly, we need to remember that all our language is metaphorical, a raft which carries us across the gap between what exists and our experience of it, from the privacy of my qualia to the experience of others and back again. Such an understanding may release us from the fixity of fundamentalism and of stuck identity. Both fundamentalism and identity betray what Buddhist thought would term "grasping", an attempt, albeit foredoomed, to impose fixity on the flow of impermanence.

To do this we will need to embrace imagination and creativity. How we imagine the world determines how we live in it. Human beings are the only species which can consistently think of things as "other" than they appear to exist, the only species with developed narrative and imagination. These capabilities enable us to work with and in a world which is not physically present, allowing us to envisage things in fresh and creative ways. I noted in the previous chapter that mindfulness based cognitive therapy points out that some aspects of this ability to imagine things as other may be unhelpful, leading us to a driven state, there termed "doing" (as opposed to "being"), which always leaves us fixated and unsatisfied, caught between what is and what could or "should" be. To avoid this, we need to find a place of balance between doing and being, imagination and ground, and always an understanding of the dangers of grasping and fixation. Jerome Bruner has shown that "through narrative, we construct, reconstruct, in some ways reinvent yesterday and tomorrow. Memory and imagination fuse in the process" (2002, p. 93). Memory requires imagination so that we do not become trapped in the past; imagination needs memory to keep its feet on the ground. Bruner continues:

The art of the possible is a perilous art. It must take heed of life as we know it, yet alienate us from it sufficiently to tempt us into thinking of alternatives beyond it. It challenges as it comforts. In the end, it has the power to change our habits of conceiving what is real, what canonical. [*ibid.*, p. 94]

This has always been the domain of the arts: to enlarge our sense of possibilities, present the familiar in new guises, engage our emotions and give us new ways to frame our stories.

Wendell Berry presents us with a gentle perspective on imagination, suggesting that "to know imaginatively is to know intimately, particularly, precisely, gratefully, reverently and with affection" (2000, p. 138). Such knowledge can re-enchant the world, restoring colour and depth. Ideas about our place in the world, and the images which express this, determine what we attend to, what questions we can ask and what answers to expect about life. Thus imagination and image are central to the controlling paradigms and structure of our world. The writer Ursula Le Guin notices an important and often overlooked fact when she writes: "The exercise of the imagination is dangerous to those who profit from the way things are because it has the power to show that the way things are is not permanent, not universal, not necessary" (2004, p. 219). Imaginative knowing, as Berry and Bruner describe, allows us to respond anew, moment by moment, rather than lazily resorting to old scripts, ignoring difference. Terrifying when felt as groundlessness, difference may be celebrated when shared practices of embodiment provide experienced foundation, inextricably linking us with community and with world. A moment's awareness of breath brings us into embodied awareness of self and non self, and of our reliance on air and world outside our skin. Imagination prevents us from reifying, from literalising, from alienating the object from its relations. Awareness awakens us to embodied experience.

As Berry demonstrates, to live creatively does not need to be interpreted in terms of the heroic quest and of superman or the professional artist. The scientist and writer David Peat recently wrote at the conclusion of his exploration of creativity: "Simply giving attention to your life may engage creativity on a full-time basis" (2000, p. 217). He suggests that we use our energy and our creativity to engage with the world directly, to merge horizons with it, and to re-animate and renew all that lies around us. "Being creative", he writes, "means giving great attention to one's whole being, to what one does and how one does it. It means taking nothing for granted and trying to see what may lie behind all the habits of body and mind" (*ibid.*, p. 218). Such attention requires mindfulness, including alertness and awareness, and the receptive openness we discussed in the last chapter, openness both to the hidden and to chance. Attention and openness form the fabric of creativity. "Accepting chance means remaining in a state of openness to the moment. That is where creativity lies" (*ibid.*, p. 221). It is an act of engagement with the world, starting with what is both most familiar and, when we really pay attention, most strange—our selves.

At the time that I write, there is much discussion in England about childhood—and the lack of it, the stress that children are under to perform and to consume. Opponents to such criticism point also to the childishness of adults and their refusal to take responsibility. Older people point to the play we enjoyed as children, when streets and fields seemed safer and toys fewer. Certainly free play encourages imagination, allowing minimal props to stand for greater objects: the tree that is a castle, the piece of wood or pebble an animal or companion. Also important is the ability to fashion our own story, fostered by hearing, reading and being listened to, and in time to write our own stories. A friend recently spoke to me of her eleven-year-old daughter in America, who had just joined a new class at the beginning of the school year. Many of her classmates were finding their new teacher very difficult, as she was asking them to write free imaginative essays on a theme she would give them. Many of the pupils had never been asked to write imaginatively before; they had merely chosen from given answers to set questions. There is without doubt wonderful practice going on in our schools and families still today, but a careful consideration of attention and imagination in education and family would be of immense value.

Imagination is essential for compassion, the ability to empathize, to imaginatively extend our own experience to that of others. Such enhanced awareness of our connectedness may help us to touch and feel com-passion, feeling-with, resonance and engagement. Stephen Batchelor speaks of the "self creation of individuation" and "world creation of social engagement" as the two poles of a culture of awakening (1997, p. 112). In the absence of absolutes, this view restores morality in the form of an increasing sensitivity, responsive to the needs of an ever-expanding variety of people and things. Such an extension springs from a sense of self as relational rather than isolated, a connection central to Buddhist Dharma. And this Dharma too must be approached both with reverence and with imagination. The Buddha had a vision which has been of value within widely and wildly different contexts, and is still of value today. But it requires imagination and creativity to interpret its beauty and truth for today. For Buddhism itself may be grasped as fundamentalism or embraced as fad. As fad it offers a new and different set of beliefs, unsullied by familiarity and all the disadvantages of our heritage. As fundamentalism it can offer a new system to shore up our ruins, a new set of beliefs to hold the darkness at bay, to cover up our lack of certainty and security, a new metanarrative with which we can cover up the cracks in the old. Both, however, are an evasion of the problem, an evasion of the first noble truth, and fail to reflect the real message of the Dharma. The flaw in fundamentalist thinking is a refusal to acknowledge context, a failure of imagination. It shows an inability to appreciate that however much something in itself may appear to be unchanging, nothing exists in isolation; it is inevitably changed by its surroundings, by causes, conditions and context. This is the central lesson of dependent origination; and remember that the historic Buddha said: "One who sees dependent origination sees the Dhamma; one who sees the Dhamma sees dependent origination."[4] The living meaning of Buddhist teachings and practices is as a path of liberation, not as an institution. We can work with our minds to change our relationship with the world. This is surely the one thing available to human—and only to human—beings. It does not mean we should see ourselves as entirely separated from our animal origins, but it is our unique potential, which we should not ignore. It also takes work and practice.

Along similar lines, the American philosopher Richard Rorty has written that anti-essentialist pragmatist philosophers see "both intellectual and moral progress not as a matter of getting closer to the True or the Good or the Right but as an increase in imaginative power. We see imagination as the cutting edge of cultural evolution, the power which—given peace and prosperity—continually operates so as to make the human future richer than the human past" (1999, p. 87). We may be—we are—merely a step in evolution, and we should not see ourselves as divorced from our animal past or in command of the future, but a lack of complete freedom is surely not a lack of any freedom. Neuroplasticity demonstrates potential. If learning and practice can generate new cells and new connection, we may practice for a happier and healthier future. We do have some freedom, some choice; we can work towards eudaimonia.

Both East and West point to a movement between the poles of freedom and constraint, personal liberation and social involvement. From both neuroscience and Buddhism comes the story of a middle way: a way forged between idealism and materialism, between constraint and freedom. We are constrained by our embodiment and our enworldedness, yet through the relative freedom of our imagination we may extend the boundaries of our understanding in ways that become embodied, instantiated in neurological language. This middle way emphasises the importance of creativity and imagination in transforming and realigning ourselves. In our present need this middle way is more than ever called for: a way that may help us to balance freedom and fixity, imagination and reality, experience and interpretation, metaphor and literality.

As noted earlier, the neuroscientist Francisco Varela observed that research has shown that there is more and more evidence that perception and imagination are very closely linked mental functions.[5] Damasio too, describes how fresh perceptual images and those reconstructed from memory have the same kind of effect. The car crash you experienced many years ago will be remembered, and the memory will cause the same reactions of fear. Experience accompanied by strong emotion forms strong memory. Understanding neuroplasticity may enable us to reconfigure traumatic memories, working carefully in a safe situation in order to de-link them from their reactive emotion, changing the hold they have on the present and the future. As Varela said, "You can learn and modify with the imagination in a physiological sense" (Goleman, 2003). Such techniques are used today both by therapists working with the effects of trauma and, more positively, by sports coaches who train their charges through imagination to win in reality.

Varela went so far as to state that the mind is fundamentally a matter of imagination and fantasy, that perception is as imaginary as imagination is perception-based; that the mind is not about representing some external state of affairs but is actively involved in the construction (he terms it the "secretion") of reality that constitutes the world (1999, p. 77; see also Appendix 1). Such co-creation moves between freedom and constraint, and the space of freedom calls for imagination and creativity to make best use of that freedom. As the title of his recent book suggests, the philosopher Daniel Dennet (2003) tells us that *Freedom Evolves*. Freedom, he says, is not an illusion but an objective phenomenon found only in the human species, a phenomenon which has had to evolve and which continues to evolve. Its evolution has depended on our abilities of reflection and communication. And with the evolution of freedom has come, inevitably, responsibility. As evolution quickens as carried by culture, there is an ever-growing need for an understanding that ethical action, freedom and happiness require practice.

From the Mahayana Buddhist perspective, religion, art and self are ultimately empty. Empty, that is, of fixed unchanging essence, a principle which appears most compatible with a contemporary Western science that presents us with the complementarity of wave and particle, and the linguistic deconstruction and deferral of the postmodern. This, I repeat, is empty, but in a different sense from that of privation. "Translating *sunyata* as Emptiness is something worse than a misuse of language; it is a spiritual infidelity." So wrote the poet Octavio Paz (quoted in Baker, 2004, p. 259). For the other face of emptiness is the abundant co-construction of dependent origination: basic emptiness, that unfindability of the single truth, is founded upon Indra's net, the multiplicity of interdependent, co-emergent and impermanent phenomena. Thus this does not leave us bereft of ways to live day by day. Under the rule of the conventional or relative truth of co-emergent, or dependent, origination, it is neither pointless nor impossible to point to a path for living well, which will support the best experiment in selfhood, even in the understanding that such an experiment is inspired by the knowledge that ultimately such a self is no self.

Trust is necessary in what is "other", non-human, and unconscious. Our safety net is the net of dependent origination, Indra's net, an interdependent whole of which we are a part. This shows both the impossibility of taking a stance outside, from which certainty may be seen, and also that there is no need for this. As the writer Terry Tempest Williams described on seeing Earthrise, "If in fact we are in free fall, we can relax, because we also know there is no ground, so no need for a parachute. If we are a part of the whole, what more do we want?" If the original meaning of the term "enthusiasm" was possession by a god or gods, by 1800 it stood for poetic ecstasy. In the absence of gods today, can we enthuse ourselves, encouraged by imagination and trust in the web of life? Can we surrender, become receptive and participant, and at least question technological thinking which has led to alienation? Can we rejoice in our unrepeatable individuality, yet hold it lightly and playfully, fulfilled in the embeddedness of context in participation, just as a scientist may be aware that the table at which she is sitting is a mass of space and moving particles, yet depends on it to support her computer?

Knowing how experience is mediated through language, we should recognize the importance of our metaphors, how experience can be changed by the horizons of expectation, theory and metaphor, just as the hedge of diamonds described at the beginning of the book turned to mud as the perspective altered. We have discussed the work of George Lakoff and Mark Johnston taking the implications of the findings of mind scientists into the sphere of language and philosophy. A very large proportion of our language, when carefully considered, is found to be metaphoric rather than literal. Through constant usage we regard it as literal, speaking through dead metaphors. To learn to re-use language consciously and imaginatively and to re-inhabit our bodies and our emotions would allow us to live creatively, and to see that such seemingly small moves will reinvigorate our worlds. To take one important example from Lakoff and Johnson: they show how many of our descriptions of discussion arise from metaphors of war (1980, p. 4). For example: "You win or lose an argument", "He attacked every weak point in my argument", "He shot down all my arguments", "His criticisms were right on target", and so on. The "argument is war" metaphor is one we live by. All the things we do in argument are structured by the concept of war. We actually do win or lose arguments. There is a verbal battle: attack, defence, counter-argument, and so on. Lakoff and Johnston suggest that we imagine a culture in which arguments are not structured by concepts of war but rather by those of dance. There would then be no sense of attacking, gaining or losing ground, but rather a sense of performance, of being balanced or aesthetically pleasing. By such conscious inhabitation, not only of language but also of selves, we may rediscover the freedom we actually have.

A Buddhist has pointed out in connection with the work of Lakoff and Johnston that perhaps one of the most pervasive metaphors is that of reality as substance (Cabezon, 1994, p. 53). This metaphor most importantly extends to the concept of self as substance. As we know, we constantly speak of the self as substantial possession or reified identity. In Western terms A. N. Whitehead (1929), propounding a metaphysical system rejecting substance in favour of process, has written of the "fallacy of misplaced concreteness", the misconception of an abstraction or concept as a concrete particular. Gregory Bateson has also described self as a false reification, an "improperly delineated part of this much larger field of interlocking processes" (1972, p. 302). Wendell Berry has perceptively described how such metaphors move imperceptibly from awareness of metaphor through equivalence to identification. All of Buddhism's theoretical models and awareness practices go towards a transposition from the concept of reality as substance to that of a re-understanding of reality as process—one which is at least to some extent observer-dependent. Mindfulness and meditation, through careful observation of experience, expose its constructed nature and contingence. The practices and rituals of Tantric Buddhism are imaginative practices in re-imagining self and world in accordance with awakening perception. As we have discussed, our conception of our selves is central to our experience, our perception of world and our morality.

Dharma practice is self-creation, but one of its unique and most important aspects is its imaginative openness to not self, the emphasis on compassion that acts as a safety net. The practice of psychotherapy too is a practice of awareness of self, particularly of the centrality today of self-image. Much of psychological unhappiness, many of the presenting problems which bring people into therapy arise when the self image causes friction with ongoing experience. Instead of seeing our selves as constructions compounded from the totality of experience, acting as what Daniel Dennet calls a "centre of narrative gravity", a provider of a sense of continuity amidst change, we identify literally, permanently and essentially with a static self image; this then causes resistance to ongoing experience which challenges it, just as a rock is rubbed against by the water flowing past. Our self serves as a point of reference. Suffering occurs from both Buddhist and psychotherapeutic perspectives when we identify with an unchanging identity of "me" not as a useful device but as a fixation. We impose arbitrary boundaries onto patterns of relationship, and then grant autonomous existence to the segments we have created. Thus we identify with a bounded persistent entity rather than living as a dynamic network of relations.

We are *both* our unique and unrepeatable selves, formed mentally and physically through the expectations and resultant neurological instantiation of our previous experience, *and* their contingency and ongoing process. Our task is to unite a fulfilment of our individual, unrepeatable matrix of inheritance and circumstance with awareness of its contingency and embeddedness in world. Our individual identity arises not because we possess autonomous essence or quality, but as the result of individual unrepeatable processes and sets of causes and conditions. Knowing the ultimate contingency of this, we can celebrate and authentically inhabit our uniqueness, knowing all others have their own constructed individuality. Without clinging, without fixation, self is consumed in its selfing, leaving no residue of separate image to be disconnected from world, to be defended from fear of its inadequacy, or pulled by desire to enlarge itself. We are neither reducible to one or all of our causes and conditions, nor are we separate from them. We are our stories, our processes, our beliefs, but we are not separate and permanent, and isolated from our world and from the causes and conditions which formed us. For, as a small child said to her father, "If my self were permanent, how could I grow up?"

Because of the difficulty of moving through the many spheres of our experience, inhabiting the many roles we play, following the rules of the many language games, we forget that they are roles and games. Our very being becomes fixated on being *some thing*, a reified identity which we must then defend from threat and build up with desire. Identity freezes connection and supports an encapsulated self, grasping a reified past and projecting a future as product rather than process. Our rich ongoing experience is narrowed into a momentary punctual self image of permanent identity, a constant attempt at repetition rather than a flexible response to changing conditions. As the world inevitably changes around us, this static identity will always be under threat, always seduced by what may strengthen it. Can we see ourselves as novelists rather than polemicists? Could we learn playfully to celebrate difference, change and creation with compassion and lightness of touch?

Our mistake has been to take our language literally and to forget the metaphors, to regard our selves literally and substantially, not to see them as constructions, creations in progress. If we hold ourselves more lightly, if we see we are our stories, we can creatively re-imagine, rewrite ourselves. Psychotherapy asks us to do this when we are suffering: to see our patterns, our identifications and our fixations, to loosen them so that we may recognise other resources, and to imagine other possibilities of choice, action and belief in order to reframe our lives and write new narratives more conducive to wellbeing. Understanding the supporting network of causes and conditions, the contingency of self, whether exposed by meditation, postmodern deconstruction or psychotherapy, may be seen as a contingency that is full of process, not as an emptiness of lack. Letting go of the literalness of our stories, we may awaken to their metaphoric truth and see that identifying ourselves with them may be confining rather than supporting. We already conceive and speak metaphorically; our error has been to forget this and take our language literally. Just as psychologically we fixate on a self image and identify with that image until it becomes a confinement, alienating us from the full openness to ongoing experience that does not "fit" this image, so we have fixated and reified our language, taking fixedly and literally what should be an imaginative process grounded in embodiment, yet imaginatively extended. Fixating ourselves in order to defend ourselves from suffering, we have only increased that suffering. Fixations bring fear in their wake: fear of what challenges them, fear of losing them, fear that they are not enough.

In pluralistic cultures it is difficult, if not impossible, any longer to foster adherence to *the* myth, the dogma. However, in the democracy of the imagination, imagination is the possession of each of us, providing freedom to creatively live our own personal narratives. Within the constraints of context and compassion there is still room for personal incarnation, still room for imaginative authentic aesthetic creation born out of close attention to our bodies, our minds, our environment and our world. Aesthesis in ancient Greek, the root of aesthetics, meant perception or sensation. We *are* our stories which are all created from the interweaving of body, mind and world. Rather than being helpless victims, let us creatively and imaginatively live our choices. Escaping from the cold hand of dead metaphors turned into unbending identifications and from the dogmas of authoritative regimes, let us consciously reforge new metaphors.

Letting go of fixation and obstacles, we may fall not into greater suffering or into nothingness, into no self and no reality, but into the net of embodiment, interconnection, metaphoric truth, adventure, humour and celebration. Caught in the endless pendulum swing of duality, essentialist opponents of this new pluralism and pragmatism point in fear to the danger of absolute relativism, a loss of all foundation for ethical behaviour, a state of anarchy. This is still to be caught in absolutism, the swing from absolute essence to absolute nothingness. Both Buddhists and scientific pragmatists are concerned with the middle ground of embodied humanity, shared practices and imaginative compassion that understands the inseparability of self and other, society and world. Buddhism itself should stand as an exemplar of the emptiness of such fears. For over two thousand years its teachings have been centrally concerned with an ethical way of living unsupported by any god or creator. They are, however, supported by a network of practices and a philosophy which teaches of our dependence upon causes and conditions which, though empty of essential nature, are not non-existent. Such emptiness is not a lack, merely an emptiness of essential being that is yet a fullness of relative and contingent being. Perhaps it is only our fear that gets in the way.

As the mind sciences bring further scientific knowledge of the ways our experience is formed, let us also explore Buddhist practices that help us subjectively understand these processes, and the stories and teachings which have long encouraged authentic and wise response to the challenges of life. Let us bring them together that we may distinguish between what is determined and what can be transformed. The good news is that some things are changeable, the most important being our own response to change. But it does take practice, and the etymology of "practice" is "to do habitually, to exercise oneself for the purpose of obtaining proficiency, with the view of acquiring a skill; to bring about and to intend". All of which emphasise that living well doesn't just happen; it is a skill, and one that needs practice. May the old and new unite to explore ways of self-cultivation and self-location in the service of happiness and well-being. If we can let go of our fear and our defended and separated selves, awareness of such impermanence and vulnerability, with humour and humility, may also increase wonder and happiness.

Notes

1. For an interesting discussion of how we have often forced new discoveries into old moulds, see Gray (2002).
2. From an article in the London newspaper *The Guardian*, 2.10.97.
3. Batchelor first discussed this in "A Democracy of the Imagination", in *Tricycle*, Vol. 4, no. 2, Winter 1994. The idea of self-creation is also discussed in more detail in the last section of Batchelor (1997).
4. *Majjhima Nikkaya*, p. 283. This quote uses the term *Dhamma*, which is Pali, the language of early Buddhism, rather than the term *Dharma*, which is Sanskrit and the term more commonly used by later Mahayana Buddhism. *Dharma* is the term I have commonly used elsewhere.
5. See Goleman, 2003, p. 285; see also Damasio, 2003, p. 57.

The enactive view

B ringing many of the recent findings of the mind sciences together, the enactive view rests on three main pillars in its challenge to our normal ways of thinking. These are *Embodiment*, *Emergence* and *Interconnection*, which includes *Intersubjectivity*. All of these headings are themselves interconnected, for the concern of the enactive approach is not to recover the comforting security of a perceiver-independent world, but to find and understand the linkages between sensory and motor systems within a perceiver-dependent world. Understanding these linkages, we may learn how best to act and live in recognition of the (re)connection of organism and environment, which we now know are bound together in reciprocal process. Enactive cognitive science, particularly in the work of the late Francisco Varela and of Evan Thompson, promotes the importance of embodiment and the inseparability of body and mind, the centrality of emergence and the inseparability of seer and seen. This reveals a state of what Buddhism has termed dependent co-arising.

In a discussion of his views, an outline for a book which sadly he never lived to complete, Varela illustrated the key point of *Embodiment* with the slogan "The mind is not in the head". He expanded this slogan to state that cognition is what he described as enactively embodied — something that is brought forth by the act of doing. This has been termed sensorimotor contingency, being a "co-determination of what seems to be outside and what seems to be inside. In other words, the world out there and what I do to find myself in that world cannot be separated" (1999, p. 73).[1]

His second key point of *Emergence* describes how local states of neuronal activity give rise to the establishment of what he terms a "global process", a subject which is neither independent of these local interactions nor reducible to them. The global state that emerges from the local rules has a different ontological status because it entails the circulation of a cognitive unity, an individual. Varela writes of mind as being an actively emergent co-determination of neural elements (local) and cognitive subject (global). As a result of the generic features of "emergence" in complex systems, one can expect two-way or reciprocal relationships between these two layers, neural events and conscious activity. These are important differences between the enactive approach and other groupings that assume a one-way causal explanatory relationship between internal neural activity and the contents of consciousness. Enactive cognitive science is concerned with allowing for and exploring the two-way traffic between global subject and local processes. Not only will neuronal activity affect conscious experience, but also conscious experience may affect neuronal activity and physicality.

Bringing together these two points of embodiment and emergence, Varela bursts through the mind-body-world divisions and writes of mind as not about representing a state of affairs but rather as the secretion of a coherent reality that constitutes a world, stating that "perception is as imaginary as imagination is perception-based" (1999, p. 77). He cites experiments which show that one can give an actively embodied organism anything at all as an excuse for sensory-motor contingencies and it will constitute a world that is shaped and formed. He speaks of a shift from the belief that there are properties necessary for the apprehension of a coherent picture of reality to the notion that almost anything may serve as an excuse to invent a reality.[2]

The third key component of this view is *intersubjectivity*, which goes beyond the co-determination of self and world to posit the co-determination of self and other. Our very fundamental self-consciousness emerges from a primordial and preverbal sense of self, found to be present in newborn infants, which is inseparably coupled to the perceptual recognition of other human beings.[3]

Research into the development of young children and primates that has shown that the very physical constitution of children can be modified at the genetic level according to the degree of love and care they receive. Further evidence for intersubjectivity is shown by research on the so-called mirror neurons, which have been seen in primates to display the same patterns of activity both when a subject accomplishes certain actions and when they observe another performing the same actions (Gallese & Goldman, 1998, pp. 493–501).

This thesis of self-other co-determination is linked to the current re-discovery of the importance of emotion in cognition that is discussed in more detail elsewhere. Affect is not only a whole-organism event but, to quote Thompson, it is "a prototypical *two-organism event*, by which I mean a prototypical *self-other event*" (2001b, p. 4). This statement occurs in a long article on the importance of empathy in the development of consciousness, both evolutionary and personal.

Following on from these points, enactive cognitive science sees that progress in studies of consciousness will require new methodology, in particular the use of nonlinear dynamic systems theory to explore the reciprocal emergent processes, since nonlinearity is a feature of two-way feedback processes. Moreover, it will require a threefold approach which can weave together the formal level of mental contents and ideation, the natural level of neural bodily process, and the subjective or experiential level, since all these levels are mutually generative and interdependent. Neurophenonmenology is a term which has been used to describe such an approach which brings together Husserlian phenomenology, neuroscientific research and contemplation from the wisdom traditions, thus addressing both first and third person views and objective and subjective aspects of consciousness. The most current and comprehensive presentation of the enactive approach appears in *Mind in Life* by Evan Thompson, which unfortunately for me, was published too late for inclusion in this summary.

Notes

1.   Information for this appendix comes largely from this paper.
2.   The sensorimotor explanation of vision, propounded by the psychologist Kevin O'Regan and the philosopher Alvin Noe, considers that vision

is not about building internal representations but is a way of acting in the world, about mastering the sensorimotor contingencies. What you see are those aspects of the scene that you are currently visually manipulating; thus seeing, attending and acting become the same thing, an enaction of world. See Blackmore, 2005b, p. 64.

3. Research for this comes from Gallagher & Meltzoff (1996) and Melzoff & Moore (1999).

The Mind and Life Institute and other resources

The Mind and Life programme was initiated in 1985 by the neuroscientist Francisco Varela and Adam Engle, an American lawyer and businessman, to set up a series of dialogues between His Holiness the Dalai Lama and Western scientists. It is dedicated today to fostering dialogue and research between modern science and the great contemplative traditions, particularly Buddhism, through meetings, research projects, publications and educational programmes. Its vision is to establish a collaboration and research partnership between modern science and Buddhism for understanding the nature of reality and investigating the mind. H.H. the Dalai Lama believes that science and Buddhism have a common objective: to serve humanity and create a better understanding of the world. He believes that science offers powerful tools for understanding the interconnectedness of life, and that such understanding provides a rationale for ethical behaviour and the protection of the environment.

The first meeting in 1987 has been followed by many others. These have mostly taken a similar format, with morning presentations by Western scientists followed by discussion in the afternoon.

The meetings have for the most part been private, with a small invited audience. Many of them have been followed by publication of a record of the event. Two translators with strong backgrounds in science, a Tibetan and a Western Buddhist, have helped the proceedings. For the majority of the meetings these have been Thupten Jinpa, who holds both Tibetan geshe degrees and a PhD in philosophy from Cambridge University, and Allan B. Wallace, a former monk in the Tibetan tradition who has a degree in physics from Amherst University.

Mind and Life I took place in Dharamsala in 1987, and was written up as *Gentle Bridges: Conversations with the Dalai Lama on the Sciences of Mind*, edited by Jeremy Hayward (Boston, MA: Shambhala, 1992).

Mind and Life II took place in October 1989 in California, with an emphasis on neuroscience. Its deliberations were published as *Consciousness at the Crossroads: Conversations with the Dalai Lama on Brain Science and Buddhism*, edited by Z. Houshmand, R. B. Livingston and B. A. Wallace (Ithaca, NY: Snow Lion, 1999).

Mind and Life III was again held in Dharamsala in 1990, and focused on the relations between emotions and health. This was published as *Healing Emotions: Conversations with the Dalai Lama on Mindfulness, Emotion and Health*, edited by Daniel Goleman (Boston, MA: Shambhala, 1997). As an outcome of this conference, the first research programme to investigate the effects of meditation on long-term meditators was set up. At this time also the Mind and Life Institute was formally constituted.

Mind and Life IV occurred in 1992, and an account of it was published as *Sleeping, Dreaming and Dying: An Exploration of Consciousness with the Dalai Lama*, edited by F. J. Varela (Boston, MA: Wisdom Publications, 1997).

Mind and Life V took place in April 1995, and the record was published as *Visions of Compassion: Western Scientists and Tibetan Buddhists Examine Human Nature*, edited by R. J. Davidson and A. Harrington (New York: Oxford University Press, 2001).

Mind and Life VI, in October 1997, moved away from the focus on mind sciences and was published as *The New Physics and Cosmology: Dialogues with the Dalai Lama*, edited by Arthur Zajonc (New York: Oxford University Press, 2004).

Mind and Life VII, continuing the theme of quantum physics, took place in June 1998 at Anton Zeilinger's laboratory at the Institut für Experimental-Physik in Innsbruck, Austria. This meeting was recorded as a story in the June 1999 issue of *Geo* magazine in Germany.

Mind and Life VIII, returning to earlier subjects, took place in March 2000, back in Dharamsala, and the record was published as *Destructive Emotions: How Can We Overcome Them*, edited by Daniel Goleman (New York: Bantam, Doubleday Dell, 2002).

Following on from this, Mind and Life IX visited the University of Wisconsin at Madison in co-operation with the Health Emotions Research Institute and the Center for Research on Mind-Body Interactions. Here participants viewed the technologies of fMRI and EEG/MEG and their use in research of meditation, perception, emotion and neural plasticity. Sadly, days after this meeting (which he was too unwell to attend other than through video link-up), long time instigator and scientific co-ordinator Francisco Varela passed away in Paris.

Mind and Life X returned to Dharamsala in October 2002, and was concerned with "The Nature of Matter, the Nature of Life"; as yet there is no publisher for the report of this conference.

Mind and Life XI was the first public meeting, and took place in Boston at MIT in September 2003, entitled "Investigating the Mind" (www.investigatingthemind.org). The proceedings have been published by Harvard University Press as *The Dali Lama at MIT*, edited by Anne Harrington & Arthur Zajonc (2006).

Mind and Life XII, which took place in Dharamsala in 2004 entitled "Neuroplasticity: The Neuronal Substrates of Learning and Transformation", was written up by Sharon Begley and was published in 2007 entitled *Train Your Mind, Change Your Brain*. Ballentine Books, New York.

Mind and Life XIII took place in November 2005 in Washington, DC entitled "Investigating the Mind: The Science and Clinical Application of Meditation". The record of this meeting is being written up by Ann Harrington and Arthur Zajonc.

Mind and Life XIV took place in April 2007 in Dharamsala around the topic of H.H. the Dalai Lama's recent book *The Universe in a Single Atom*, and was chaired by Arthur Zajonc. This was followed in September 2007 by a meeting in Berlin on "Attention and Consciousness". A Mind and Life Education Research Network has been set up, and held its first meeting in July 2006. Believing that if meditation is beneficial, the earlier it is encountered the better, it is concerned with attempts to introduce meditation early in life into the education system. The Mind and Life meeting for 2008 will then have the subject of education.

Building on the research begun in 1990, a decision was made to sponsor serious research into the effects of meditation, to be published in authoritative peer-reviewed scientific journals. Sustained research on meditation and brain function is taking place at CREA in Paris, at the University of Wisconsin at Madison (with Professor Richard Davidson), at Harvard University, as well as at the University of California, both at Berkeley and at San Francisco. Arising out of Mind and Life VIII on "Destructive Emotions", Paul Ekman of UCSF and colleagues inaugurated a project entitled "Cultivating Emotional Balance", designed to evaluate the effectiveness of a training programme to increase awareness and management of emotional behaviour. Participants, teachers in a stressful occupation, were trained in skills such as meditation and the recognition of emotional communication by facial expression, and taught strategies to counteract negative emotions. The clinical trial for this began in early 2005. An account published in *Psychology Today* in September 2006 (K. Ellison, "Managing Your Own Mind") reports that initial results are positive, showing that less than thirty minutes of meditation daily significantly improved mood.

To encourage scientific research the Mind and Life Summer Research Institute has been set up to advance collaborative research amongst behavioural scientists, neuroscientists and biomedical researchers based on a process of inquiry, dialogue and collaboration with Buddhist scholars and contemplative practitioners. Its

long-term objective is to train a new generation of scientists interested in exploring the potential influences of meditation and other
such contemplative practices on mind, behaviour, brain function
and health, so that a collaborative research programme may be
set up by informed individuals who, through their own intensive
training and practice, have developed an experiential first-person
knowledge and control of their own mental processes. Arising from
the Summer Institutes, various F. J. Varela Research Awards have
been given to support chosen projects put forward by graduates.
The Mind and Life Institute has also instigated summer retreats to
encourage the practice of meditation and underline its relevance
to happiness and wellbeing. In summer 2006, a retreat entitled
"The Buddha, the Brain and the Science of Happiness" took place
at Garrison, New York, led by Mingyur Rinpoche, assisted by the
scientists Richard Davidson, Antoine Lutz and Al Shapere. Other
retreats have been organised in conjunction with the Insight Meditation organization.

A breakthrough in public recognition came with a report from
the Proceedings of the National Academy of Sciences in November
2004, describing the results of studies set up by the Mind and Life
IX meeting in Madison in 2001. This report, entitled "Long Term
Meditators Self-Induce High Amplitude Gamma Synchrony during
Mental Practice", suggested that mental training might induce both
short- and long-term changes to the brain. It describes meditation,
or mental training, as a process of familiarization with one's own
mental life leading to long-lasting changes in cognition and emotion.
This has led to a vast increase in public and journalistic interest in the
subject. In the first three months of 2005, articles concerning Richard
Davidson's work appeared in *The Washington Post*, *The Financial
Times*, and *National Geographic* and *Time* magazines. The *Time* story,
entitled "The Biology of Joy", suggested that happiness is a physical
state of the brain, and one which can be deliberately induced. The
National Geographic cover story was an in-depth look at the human
brain entitled "What's in Your Mind?" and refers both to Davidson's
work and to the Cultivating Emotional Balance project.

In November 2005 an estimated 14,000 people listened to H.H.
the Dalai Lama at a lecture presented to the Society for Neuroscience
in Washington DC, during which he urged neuroscientists not to
discount the role of Buddhist knowledge of the brain, especially with

respect to the benefits of meditation. Earlier, many scientists had signed a petition against the invitation for the Dalai Lama to address the meeting, concerned about the mixing of religion and science, and also possibly with some political motivation (many of the protesters were originally from China). However, on the day the speech was well received and well reported, and there was little or no outcry.

A further article in *Time* magazine in January 2006, entitled "How to Get Smarter One Breath at a Time", concerned meditation, showing that it not only reduces stress but reshapes the brain, altering it in ways that appear to increase attention span, sharpen focus and improve memory.

Mind and Life Institute
2805 Lafayette Drive
Boulder, CO 80305
USA

www.mindandlife.org
www.investigatingthemind.org
info@mindandlife.org

Other Resources

Center for Mindfulness In Medicine, Healthcare & Society (CFM)

Established in 1995, the Center for Mindfulness (CFM) is an outgrowth of the acclaimed Stress Reduction Clinic, founded by Jon Kabat-Zinn in 1979. Under the direction of Dr. Saki Santorelli, the CFM is a multi-dimensional center in the Division of Preventive and Behavioral Medicine, within the Department of Medicine at the University of Massachusetts Medical School. Since 1979, when the Stress Reduction Clinic was founded, the Center for Mindfulness has been a leader in mind-body medicine, pioneering the integration of mindfulness meditation and other mindfulness-based practices into mainstream medicine through patient care, research, medical and professional education, and to the larger society through a broad range of outreach and public service initiatives.

The Stress Reduction Program—the oldest and largest academic medical center-based stress reduction program in the world—has been featured in the Bill Moyers' PBS documentary Healing and the Mind and in the book of the same title, on Oprah, NBC Dateline, ABC's Chronicle, and in various national print media. It is also the subject of Jon Kabat-Zinn's best-selling book, *Full Catastrophe Living: Using the Wisdom of Your Body and Mind to Face Stress, Pain, and Illness* (Delta, 1990) and Saki Santorelli's book, *Heal Thy Self: Lessons on Mindfulness in Medicine* (Random House, 1999). www.umassmed.edu/cfm

The Institute of HeartMath

The Institute of HeartMath is a recognized global leader in researching the critical link among emotions, heart-brain communication and cognitive function. IHM's 15 years of research, with the insight of founder Doc Childre, into heart intelligence is the foundation of practical, scientifically validated solutions, aimed at empowering people to reduce stress, fine-tune performance in all areas of their lives and foster greater health, well-being and their innermost sense of self. www.heartmath.org

Heartwood Institute for Neuroscience and Contemplative Wisdom

Mission: To offer skillful means for changing the brain to benefit the whole person—and all beings in a world too full of war. It draws on psychology, neurology, and the great contemplative traditions for tools that anyone can use in daily life for greater happiness, love, effectiveness, and wisdom.

Founders are Rick Hanson, PhD and Rick Mendius, MD. Dr Hanson is a psychologist, Dr. Mendius is a nurologist, and both are long-time Buddhist practioners. They teach and write extensively, for both professionals and the public, about translating the latest brain science into practical methods for personal well-being and spiritual development. The institute provides a newsletter, Wise Brain Bulletin—Free email subscriptions available from their website and Train Your Brain, an ongoing course which people can enter at any time, teaching brain-based methods for steady awareness, wholesome feelings, good intentions, a caring heart, and wise action. www.wisebrain.org

The Karuna Institute

The Karuna Institute in Devon, UK, offers MA and professional training in Core Process Psychothereapy and Craniosacral Biodynamics. Its courses are deeply influenced by Buddhist principles and worldview.
www.karuna-institute.co.uk

Mindful Awareness Research Centre (MARC)

Part of the Semel Institute for Neuroscience and Human Behavior at UCLA, this centre is dedicated to evaluating and disseminating the most appropriate and effective Mindful Awareness Practices (MAPS) to foster well-being across the lifespan jn clinical and non-clinical settings, cope with the mounting stresses of daily urban life and assist people to be more self-aware and compassionate individuals. www.marc.ucla.edu

Mindfulness-based Cognitive Therapy (MBCT)

Mindfulness-based Cognitive Therapy (MBCT) was developed by Zindel Segal, Mark Williams and John Teasdale, based on Jon Kabat-Zinn's Mindfulness-based Stress Reduction programme. The MBCT programme was designed specifically to help people who suffer repeated bouts of depression.
www.mbct.co.uk

Naropa University

Naropa University in Boulder, Colorado offers an MA Psychology programme in Contemplative Psychothereapy, a clinical training rooted in Buddhist teachings.
www.naropa.edu/academics/graduate/psychology/macp/index.cfm

BIBLIOGRAPHY

Abe, M., & Waddell, N. (2002). *The Heart of Dogen's Shobogenzo*. Albany, NY: SUNY.

Baker, I. (2004). *The Heart of the World*. New York: Penguin.

Batchelor, S. (1979). *A Guide to the Bodhisattva's Way of Life*. Dharamsala: Library of Tibetan Works and Archives.

Batchelor, S. (1994). A Democracy of the Imagination. *Tricycle* 4 no. 2.

Batchelor, S. (1997). *Buddhism Without Beliefs*. New York: Riverhead.

Batchelor, S. (2000). *Verses from the Center*. New York: Riverhead.

Batchelor, S. (2004). *Living with the Devil*. New York: Riverhead.

Bateson, G. (1972). *Steps to an Ecology of Mind*. London: Chandler.

Bateson, M. C. (1989). *Composing a Life*. New York: Grove, Atlantic.

Bateson, M. C. (1994). *Peripheral Vision*. New York: Harper Collins.

Begley, S. (2007). *Train Your Mind Change Your Brain*. New York: Ballentine Books.

Benson, C. (2001). *The Cultural Psychology of Self*. London: Routledge.

Benyus, J. (1997). *Biomimicry*. New York: William Morrow.

Berry, W. (2000). *Life is a Miracle*. New York: Counterpoint.

Blackmore, S. (2005a). *Conversations on Consciousness*. Oxford: Oxford University Press.

Blackmore, S. (2005b). *Consciousness. A Very Short Introduction*. Oxford: Oxford University Press.

Broks, P. (2003). *Into the Silent Land*. London: Atlantic Books.

Bruner, J. (1990). *Acts of Meaning*. Cambridge, MA: Harvard University Press.

Bruner, J. (2002). *Making Stories*. New York: Farrer, Strauss & Giroux.

Byrom, T. (Translator). *Dhammapada*. London: Wildwood House, 1976.

Cabezon, J. (1994). *Buddhism and Language*. Albany, NY: SUNY.

Campbell, J. (1969). *The Flight of the Wild Gander*. New York: Viking.

Capra, F. (1976). *The Tao of Physics*. London: Fontana.

Carlyle, T. (1831). *Sartor Resartus*. London: Oxford University Press, 1999.

Childs, C. (2002). *Soul of Nowhere*. Seattle, WA: Sasquatch Books.

Chomsky, N. (2000). *New Horizons in the Study of Language and Mind*. Cambridge: Cambridge University Press.

Chugani et al. (2001). Local brain functional activity following early deprivation: a study of post-institutionalised Romanian orphans. *Neuroimage 14*.

Claxton, G. (Ed.) (1986). *Beyond Therapy*. London: Wisdom.

Claxton, G. (1997). *Hare Brain Tortoise Mind*. London: Fourth Estate.

Claxton, G. (2005). *The Wayward Mind*. London. Little Brown.

Colegate, I. (2002). *A Pelican in the Wilderness*. London: Harper Collins.

Coltart, N. (1992). *Slouching Towards Bethlehem*. London: Free Association Books.

Connolly, C. (Palinurus) (1944). *The Unquiet Grave*. London: Hamish Hamilton.

Cozolino, L. (2002). *The Neuroscience of Psychotherapy*. New York: Norton.

Cozolino, L. (2006). *The Neuroscience of Human Relationships*. New York: Norton.

Dalai Lama, & Cutler, H. C. (1998). *The Art of Happiness*. New York: Riverhead.

Dalai Lama (1999). *Ethics for a New Millenium*. New York: Riverhead.

Damasio, A. (1994). *Descartes' Error*. New York: Putnam.

Damasio, A. (1999). *The Feeling of What Happens*. New York: Harcourt Brace.

Damasio, A. (2003). *Looking for Spinoza*. Orlando, FL: Harcourt.

Daniel, J. (2005). *Rogue River Journal*. Washington, DC: Shoemaker & Hoard.

Davidson, R. J., & Harrington, A. (Eds.) (2001). *Visions of Compassion*. New York: Oxford University Press.

Dennet, D. (2003). *Freedom Evolves*. London: Allen Lane, Penguin.

Dillard, A. (1974). *Pilgrim at Tinker Creek*. New York: Harper Collins.

Donaldson, M. (1992). *Human Minds*. London: Allen Lane, Penguin.

Doty, M. (2001). *Still Life With Oysters and Lemon*. Boston, MA: Beacon.

Dylan, B. (2004). *Chronicles I*. New York: Simon & Schuster.

Edelman, G. (1992). *Bright Air, Brilliant Fire*. London: Allen Lane, Penguin.

Edelman, G. (2004). *Wider than the Sky*. New Haven, CT: Yale University Press.

Ekman, P., & Davidson, R. (Eds.) (1994). *The Nature of Emotion*. New York: Oxford University Press.

Ekman, P. (2003). *Emotions Revealed*. New York: Times Books.

Elbert, T. et al. (1995). Increased cortical representation of the fingers of the left hand in string players. *Science 270*: 305–307.

Engler, J. (1984). Therapeutic Aims in Psychotherapy and Meditation. In: *Journal of Transpersonal Psychology 16*: 25–61. Revised as "Being Somebody and Being Nobody". In: J. Safran (Ed.), *Psychoanalysis and Buddhism*. Somerville, MA: Wisdom, 2003.

Epstein, M. (2005). *Open to Desire*. New York: Gotham Books.

Flanagan, O. (2002). *The Problem of the Soul*. New York: Basic Books.

Fremantle, F. (2000). *Luminous Emptiness*. Boston, MA: Shambhala.

Freud, S. (1912). Recommendations to Physicians Pracising Psychoanalysis. In: *SE 12*.

Freud, S. (1923). The Ego and the Id. In: *SE 19*.

Fromm, E., Suzuki, D.T., & de Martino, R. (1970). *Zen Buddhism and Psychoanalysis*. New York: Harper Collins.

Galin, D. (2003). The concepts "self," "person" and "I" in Western psychology and in Buddhism. In: B. A. Wallace (Ed.), *Buddhism and Science: Breaking New Ground*. New York: Columbia University Press.

Gallagher, S., & Meltzoff, A. (1996). The earliest sense of self and others: Merleau-Ponty and recent developmental studies. *Philosophical Psychology, 9*.

Gallese, V. & Goldman, A. (1998). Mirror Neurons and the Simulation Theory of Mind-Reading. *Trends in Cognitive Sciences, 12*: 493–501.

Gallese, V. (2000). The "Shared Manifold" Hypothesis. *Journal of Consciousness Studies, 8*: 5–7.

Gallese, V., Keysers, C., & Rizzoli, G. (2004). A Unifying View of the Basis of Social Cognition. *Trends in Cognitive Sciences, 8*: 396–403.

Gazzaniga, M. (1998). The Neuronal Platonist. *Journal of Consciousness Studies, 5/6*.

Gazzaniga, M. (2005). *The Ethical Brain*. Washington, DC: Dana Press.

Geertz, C. (2000). *Available Light*. Princeton, NJ: Princeton University Press.

Gendlin, E. (1981). *Focusing*. Toronto: Bantam.

Gendlin, E. (1996). *Focusing-Oriented Psychotherapy*. New York: Guilford.

Gerhardt, S. (2004). *Why Love Matters*. Hove: Brunner/Routledge.

Goleman, D. (Ed.) (1988). *The Meditative Mind*. Los Angeles: Tarcher.

Goleman, D. (1995). *Emotional Intelligence*. New York: Bantam.

Goleman, D. (2003). *Healing Emotions*. Boston, MA: Shambhala.

Goleman, D. (2003). *Destructive Emotions*. London: Bloomsbury.

Gray, J. (2002). *Straw Dogs*. London: Granta.

Greenfield, S. (2000). *The Private Life of the Brain*. London: Allen Lane, Penguin.

Hamilton, S. (1996). *Identity and Experience*. London: Luzac.

Hanna, R. & Thompson, E. (2003). The Mind-Body-Body Problem. In: *Theoria et Historia Scientiarum: International Journal for Interdisciplinary Studies, 7(1)*: 24–44.

Harraway, D. (1991). *Simians, Cyborgs & Women*. London: Free Association Books.

Harrington, A. & Zajonc, A., (Eds.) (2006). *The Dalai Lama at MIT*. Cambridge, MA & London: Harvard University Press.

Heat Moon, W. L. (1982). *Blue Highways*. New York: Little Brown (1983).

Heidegger, M. (1977). *The Question Concerning Technology*. New York: Harper.

Heine, S. (1997). *The Zen Poetry of Dogen*. New York: Tuttle.

Horgan, J. (2003). *Rational Mysticism*. New York: Houghton Mifflin.

Hubel, D. H., & Wiesel, T. N. (1964). Effects of Monocular Deprivation in Kittens. *Naunyn-Schmiedeberg's Archives of Pharmacology, 248/6*: 492–497.

James, W. (1890). *The Principles of Psychology*. Cambridge, MA: Harvard University Press, 1981.

Johnson, S. (2004). *Mind Wide Open*. New York: Scribner.

Johnston, M. (1995). *Moral Imagination*. Chicago, IL: University of Chicago.

Jung, C. G. (1958). *Collected Works, Vol. 11*. London: Routledge.

Kabat Zinn, J. (1990). *Full Catastrophe Living*. New York. Dell Publishing.

Kabat Zinn, J. (1994). *Wherever You Go, There You Are*. New York: Hyperion.

Kant, I. (1949). *Fundamental Principles of the Metaphysic of Morals*. New York: Prentice Hall.

Keleman, S. (1999). *Myth and the Body*. Berkeley, CA: Center Press.

Klein, A. C. (1995). *Meeting the Great Bliss Queen*. Boston MA: Beacon.

Kosko, B. (1994). *Fuzzy Logic*. London: Flamingo.

Lacan, J. (1977). *Ecrits*. London: Tavistock.

Lakoff, G., & Johnston, M. (1980). *Metaphors We Live By*. Chicago. IL: University of Chicago. (Reprinted 2003.)

Lakoff, G., & Johnston, M. (1999). *Philosophy in the Flesh*. New York: Perseus.

Layard, R. (2005). *Happiness: Lessons from a New Science*. London: Penguin.

Le Guin, U. (2004). *The Wave in the Mind*. Boston, MA: Shambhala.

Libet, B. (1999). Do we have free will? *Journal of Consciousness Studies, 6*: 47–57.

Lodge, D. (2002). *Consciousness and the Novel*. Cambridge, MA: Harvard University Press.

Lott, T. (1996). *The Scent of Dried Roses*. London: Viking.

Low, J. (1999). "The Structures of Suffering: Tibetan Buddhist and Cognitive Analytic Approaches." In G. Watson, S. Batchelor & G. Claxton (Eds.), *The Psychology of Awakening*. London: Rider.

Loy, D. (1988). *NonDuality*. New Haven: Yale University Press.

Lyotard, J-F. (1986). *The Postmodern Condition*. Manchester: Manchester University Press.

Magid, B. (2002). *Ordinary Mind*. Boston, MA: Wisdom.

Magid, B. (2003). Your Ordinary Mind. In: J. Safran (Ed.), *Psychoanalysis and Buddhism*. Somerville, MA: Wisdom.

Maslow, A. (1962, revised 1968). *Towards a Psychology of Being*. Princeton, NJ: Van Nostrand.

Meany, M. J. et al. (1996). Early environmental regulation of forebrain glucocorticoid receptor gene expression: Implications for adrenocortical responses to stress. *Developmental Neuroscience, 18*: 49–72.

Meltzoff, A., & Moore, M. K. (1999). Infant intersubjectivity: broadening the dialogue to include imitation, identity and intention. In: S. Braten (Ed.), *Intersubjective Communication and Emotion in Early Ontogeny*. Cambridge: Cambridge University Press.

Merton, T. (1997). *Dancing in the Water of Life*. New York: Harper Collins.

Metzinger, T. (2004). *Being No One*. MIT Press.

Montaigne, M. de (1580). *The Complete Essays*. London: Penguin, 1993.

Nagatomo, S. (1992) *Attunement Through the Body*. Albany, NY: SUNY.

Nhat Hanh, T. (1988a). *The Heart of Understanding*. Berkeley, CA: Parallax Press.

Nhat Hanh, T. (1988b). *The Sutra on the Full Awareness of Breathing*. Berkeley, CA: Parallax Press.

Nhat Hanh, T. (1990). *Transformation and Healing*. Berkeley, CA: Parallax Press.

Norretranders, T. (1998). *The User Illusion*. New York: Viking.

Olendzki, A. (2003). Buddhist Psychology. In: S. R. Segall (Ed.), *Encountering Buddhism*. Albany, NY: SUNY.

Peat, F. D. (2000). *The Blackwinged Night*. New York: Perseus.

Pert, C. (1997). *Molecules of Emotion*. New York: Scribner.

Rhys Davids, C. A. F. (Trs.) (1923, 1974). *Dhamma-Sangani. A Buddhist Manual of Psychological Ethics*. London: Pali Text Society.

Rorty, R. (1999). *Philosophy and Social Hope*. London: Penguin.

Sacks, O. (1973). *Awakenings*. London: Duckworth. (Revised London: Pelican, 1976).

Safran, J. (Ed.) (2003). *Psychoanalysis and Buddhism*. Somerville, MA: Wisdom.

Santideva. *A Guide to the Bodhisattva's Way of Life*. Dharamsala: Library of Tibetan Works & Archives. 1979.

Schore, A. N. (1994). *Affect Regulation and the Origin of the Self*. Hillsdale, NJ: Lawrence Erlbaum.

Schore, A. N. (2001a). The Effects of a Secure Attachment Relationship on Right Brain Development. *Infant Mental Health Journal, 22*: 7–60, reprinted at www.trauma-pages.com

Schore, A. N. (2001b). The Effects of Early Relational Trauma on Right Brain Development, Affect Regulation and Infant Mental Health. *Infant Mental Health Journal, 22*: 201–260, reprinted at www.trauma-pages.com

Schore, A. N. (2002). Dysregulation of the Right Brain. *Australia and New Zealand Journal of Psychiatry, 36*: 9–30.

Schore, A. N. (2003a). *Affect Regulation and the origin of the Self*. New York: Norton.

Schore, A. N. (2003b). *Affect Dysregulation and Disorders of the Self* and *Affect Regulation and the Repair of the Self*. (2 vols.) New York: Norton.

Schore, A. N. (2004). A Neuropsychoanalytical Viewpoint: Commentary on paper by Stephen Knobloch: Body Rhythms and the Unconscious, toward an understanding of clinical attention. http://www.psybc.com/paper_info.php?paper_id=150

Schore, A. N. (2005). Attachment and Affect Regulation and the Developing Brain. *Pediatrics in Review, 26/6*. Affect Regulation and Infant Mental Health. Reprinted at www.trauma-pages.com

Searle, J. (1998). Do We Understand Consciousness? *Journal of Consciousness Studies, 5/6*: 718.

Segal, Z. V., Williams, J. M. G., & Teasdale, J. D. (2002). *Mindfulness-based Cognitive Therapy for Depression*. New York: Guilford Press.

Segall, S. R. (Ed.) (2003). *Encountering Buddhism*. Albany, NY: SUNY.

Servan-Schreiber, D. (2004). *Healing Without Freud or Prozac*. London: Rodale.

Sewell, L. (1999). *Sight and Sensibility*. New York: Jeremy Tarcher/Putnam.

Siegel, D. J. (2001). *The Developing Mind*. New York: Guilford Press.

Siegel, D. J. (2007). *The Mindful Brain*. New York & London: Norton.

Sojourner, M. (2002). *Bonelight*. Reno, NV: University of Nevada.

Sprung, M. (1979). *The Lucid Exposition of the Middle Way*. London: Routledge & Kegan Paul.

Sprung, M. (1994). *After Truth*. Albany, NY: SUNY.

Stevens, V. (nd). Reading the language of the Right Brain. http://www.psybc.com/paper_display.php?paper_id=125

Strawson, G. (1999). Self and the SESMET. *Journal of Consciousness Studies, 6.*

Suzuki, D. T. (1963). *The Essentials of Zen Buddhism*. London. Putnam.

Taylor, C. (1989). *Sources of the Self*. Cambridge, MA: Harvard University Press.

Thompson, E. (Ed.) (2001a). *Between Ourselves*. Exeter: Imprint Academic.

Thompson, E. (2001b) Empathy and Consciousness. In: E. Thompson (Ed.), *Between Ourselves*. Exeter: Imprint Academic.

Thompson, E. (2003). *The Problem of Consciousness*. Calgary: Alberta: University of Calgary.

Thompson, E. (2007). *Mind in Life*. Cambridge, MA & London: The Belknap Press of Harvard University Press.

Van Gulick, R. (2001). Reduction, Emergence and Other Recent Options on the Mind/Body Problem. *Journal of Consciousness Studies, 8*: 1–34.

Varela, F. J., Thompson, E. & Rosch, E. (1991). *The Embodied Mind*. MIT Press.

Varela, F. J. (1999). Steps to a Science of Inter-being. In: G. Watson, S. Batchelor & G. Claxton (Eds.), *The Psychology of Awakening*. London: Rider.

Varela, F. J., & Depraz, N. (2003). Imagining. In: A. B. Wallace (Ed.), *Buddhism and Science*. New York: Columbia University Press.

Wallace, B. A. (2002). *The Taboo of Subjectivity*. Oxford. Oxford University Press.

Wallace, B. A. (Ed.) (2003). *Buddhism and Science: Breaking New Ground*. New York: Columbia University Press.

Walsh, R. & Vaughan, F. (Eds.) (1980). *Beyond Ego*. Los Angeles: Tarcher.

Watson, G., Batchelor, S. & Claxton, G. (Eds.) (1999). *The Psychology of Awakening*. London: Rider.

Watson, G. (2000). *The Resonance of Emptiness*. London: Routledge Curzon.

Watson, J. (1925). *Behaviorism*. New York: Norton.

Welwood, J. (Ed.) (1978). *The Meeting of the Ways*. New York: Schocken.

Welwood, J. (Ed.) (1983). *Awakening the Heart*. Boston, MA: Shambhala.

Westen, D. (1997). Towards a clinically and empirically sound theory of motivation. *Int. J. Psychoanal, 78*: 521–548.

Whitehead, A. N. (1929). *Process and Reality*. New York: Free Press, 1979.

Wilber, K., Engler, J., & Brown, D. P. (1986). *Transformations of Consciousness*. Boston, MA: Shambhala.

Williams, M., Teasdale, J., Segal, Z., & Kabat-Zinn, J. (2007). *The Mindful Way Through Depression*. New York: Guilford Press.

Williams, T. T. (2001, 2002). *Red*. New York: Random House.

Winnicott, D. (1971). *Playing and Reality*. London: Tavistock. (Republished London: Routledge, 1991.)

Winterson, J. (1995). *Art Objects*. London: Cape.

Wittgenstein, L. (1921). *Tractatus Logico-Philosophicus*. London: Routledge, 2001.

Wittgenstein, L. (1967). *Zettel*. Oxford: Blackwell, 1981.

Yuasa, Y. (1987). *The Body*. Albany, NY: SUNY.

Yuasa, Y. (1993). *The Body, Self-Cultivation and Ki Energy*. Albany, NY: SUNY.

INDEX

Please remember that this is a library book,
and that it belongs only temporarily to each
person who uses it. Be considerate. Do
not write in this, or any, library book.